Occupational Therapy
Practice Guidelines *for*

Children and Adolescents With Autism

Scott D. Tomchek, PhD, OTR/L, FAOTA
Assistant Professor of Pediatrics
Chief Occupational Therapist and Assistant Director
Weisskopf Child Evaluation Center
University of Louisville
School of Medicine
Department of Pediatrics

Jane Case-Smith, EdD, OTR/L, BCP, FAOTA
Professor
Division of Occupational Therapy
School of Allied Medical Professions
The Ohio State University

AOTA
PRESS

The American
Occupational Therapy
Association, Inc.

Vision Statement

AOTA advances occupational therapy as the pre-eminent profession in promoting the health, productivity, and quality of life of individuals and society through the therapeutic application of occupation.

Mission Statement

The American Occupational Therapy Association advances the quality, availability, use, and support of occupational therapy through standard-setting, advocacy, education, and research on behalf of its members and the public.

AOTA Staff

Frederick P. Somers, *Executive Director*
Christopher M. Bluhm, *Chief Operating Officer*

Chris Davis, *Director, AOTA Press*
Ashley Hofmann, *Production Editor*
Victoria Davis, *Editorial Assistant*

Beth Ledford, *Director, Marketing and Member Communications*
Emily Harlow, *Technology Marketing Specialist*
Jennifer Folden, *Marketing Specialist*

The American Occupational Therapy Association, Inc.
4720 Montgomery Lane
Bethesda, MD 20814
Phone: 301-652-AOTA (2682)
TDD: 800-377-8555
Fax: 301-652-7711
www.aota.org

To order: 1-877-404-AOTA (2682)

Disclaimers

This publication is designed to provide accurate and authoritative information in regard to the subject matter covered. It is sold or distributed with the understanding that the publisher is not engaged in rendering legal, accounting, or other professional service. If legal advice or other expert assistance is required, the services of a competent professional person should be sought.
—*From the Declaration of Principles jointly adopted by the American Bar Association and a Committee of Publishers and Associations*

It is the objective of the American Occupational Therapy Association to be a forum for free expression and interchange of ideas. The opinions expressed by the contributors to this work are their own and not necessarily those of the American Occupational Therapy Association.

ISBN-10: 1-56900-276-2
ISBN-13: 978-1-56900-276-6
Library of Congress Control Number: 2009925192

Design by Sarah Ely and Michael Melletz
Composition by Maryland Composition, White Plains, MD
Printing by Automated Graphics Systems, White Plains, MD

Citation: Tomchek, S. D., & Case-Smith, J. (2009). *Occupational therapy practice guidelines for children and adolescents with autism.* Bethesda, MD: AOTA Press.

Contents

Appendixes

References

Figures, Tables, and Boxes Used in This Publication

■ ■ ■

Acknowledgments

The authors for this Practice Guideline are
Scott D. Tomchek, PhD, OTR/L, FAOTA
Assistant Professor of Pediatrics, Chief Occupational
    Therapist and Assistant Director
Weisskopf Child Evaluation Center
University of Louisville, School of Medicine,
    Department of Pediatrics

Jane Case-Smith, EdD, OTR/L, BCP, FAOTA
Professor
Division of Occupational Therapy; School of Allied
    Medical Professions
The Ohio State University

The issue editor for this Practice Guideline is
Marian Arbesman, PhD, OTR/L
President, ArbesIdeas, Inc.
Consultant, AOTA Evidence-Based Practice Project
Clinical Assistant Professor, Department of
    Rehabilitation Science
State University of New York at Buffalo

The series editor for the Practice Guideline series is
Deborah Lieberman, MHSA, OTR/L, FAOTA
Program Director, Evidence-Based Practice Project
Staff Liaison to the Commission on Practice
American Occupational Therapy Association

The authors would like to acknowledge the following
individuals for their contributions to the evidence-
based literature review:
Marian Arbesman, PhD, OTR/L
Jane Case-Smith, EdD, OTR/L, BCP, FAOTA
Marian Scheinholtz, MS, OT/L.

The authors would like to acknowledge and thank the
following individuals for their participation in the con-
tent review and development of this publication:
Heather Miller Kuhaneck, MS, OTR/L
Patricia D. LaVesser, PhD, OTR/L
Renee L. Watling, PhD, OTR/L
Sandra Schefkind, MS, OTR/L
Tim Nanof, MSW
V. Judith Thomas, MGA.

■ ■ ■

Occupational Therapy Practice Guidelines for Children and Adolescents With Autism

Purpose and Use of This Publication

Practice guidelines have been widely developed in response to the health care reform movement in the United States. Such guidelines can be a useful tool for improving the quality of health care, enhancing consumer satisfaction, promoting appropriate use of services, and reducing costs. The American Occupational Therapy Association (AOTA), which represents the interests of 140,000 occupational therapists, occupational therapy assistants, and students of occupational therapy, is committed to providing information to support decision making that promotes high-quality health care and wellness and educational systems that are affordable and accessible to all.

Using an evidence-based perspective and key concepts from the *Occupational Therapy Practice Framework: Domain and Process* (AOTA, 2008b), this guideline provides an overview of the occupational therapy process for children and adolescents with autism spectrum disorder (ASD). It defines the occupational therapy domain, process, and intervention that occur within the boundaries of acceptable practice. This guideline does not discuss all possible methods of care, and while it does recommend some specific methods of care, the occupational therapist makes the ultimate judgment regarding the appropriateness of a given procedure in light of a specific client's circumstances and needs.

It is the intention of AOTA, through this publication, to help occupational therapists and occupational therapy assistants, as well as individuals who manage, reimburse, or set policy regarding occupational therapy services, understand the contribution of occupational therapy in treating children and adolescents with ASD. This guideline also can serve as a reference for parents, school administrators, educators, and other school staff; health care facility managers; education and health care regulators; third-party payers; and managed care organizations. This document may be used in any of the following ways:

- To assist occupational therapists and occupational therapy assistants in communicating about their services to external audiences
- To assist other health care practitioners, teachers, and program administrators in determining whether referral for occupational therapy services would be appropriate
- To assist third-party payers in understanding the medical necessity for occupational therapy services for children and adolescents with ASD
- To assist health and education planning teams in determining the developmental and educational need for occupational therapy
- To assist legislators, third-party payers, and administrators in understanding the professional education, training, and skills of occupational therapists and occupational therapy assistants
- To assist program developers, administrators, legislators, and third-party payers in understanding the scope of occupational therapy services

- To assist program evaluators and policy analysts in determining outcome measures for analyzing the effectiveness of occupational therapy intervention
- To assist policy, education, and health care benefit analysts in understanding the appropriateness of occupational therapy services for children and adolescents with ASD
- To assist occupational therapy educators in designing appropriate curricula that incorporate the role of occupational therapy with children and adolescents with ASD.

The introduction to this guideline includes a brief discussion of the domain and process of occupational therapy. This discussion is followed by a detailed description of the occupational therapy process for children and adolescents with ASD. Next is a summary of the results of systematic reviews of evidence from the scientific literature regarding best practices in occupational therapy intervention for this population. Finally, appendixes contain additional information for occupational therapists and occupational therapy assistants, relating to sensory and motor issues in autism, the methodology used in the evidence-based literature review, and example coding for occupational therapy services and other resources related to this topic.

Domain and Process of Occupational Therapy

Occupational therapists' expertise lies in their knowledge of occupation and of how engaging in occupations can be used to improve human performance and ameliorate the effects of disease and disability (AOTA, 2008b).

In 2002, the AOTA Representative Assembly adopted the *Occupational Therapy Practice Framework:* *Domain and Process.* Informed by the previous *Uniform Terminology for Occupational Therapy* (AOTA, 1979, 1989, 1994) and the World Health Organization's (2001) *International Classification of Functioning, Disability, and Health,* the *Framework* outlines the profession's domain and the process of service delivery within this domain. In 2008, the *Framework* was updated as part of the standard 5-year review cycle. The revisions included in the second edition focused on refining the document to reflect language and concepts relevant to current and emerging occupational therapy practice.

Domain

A profession's *domain* articulates its members' sphere of knowledge, societal contribution, and intellectual or scientific activity. The occupational therapy profession's domain centers on helping others participate in daily life activities. The broad term that the profession uses to describe daily life activities is *occupation.* As outlined in the *Framework,* occupational therapists and occupational therapy assistants[1] work collaboratively with clients to support health and participation through engagement in occupation (see Figure 1). This overarching mission circumscribes the profession's domain and emphasizes the important ways in which environmental and life circumstances influence the manner in which people carry out their occupations. Key aspects of the domain of occupational therapy are defined in Figure 2.

Process

Many professions use the process of evaluating, intervening, and targeting outcomes that is outlined in the *Framework.* Occupational therapy's application of this process is made unique, however, by its focus on occupation (see Figure 3). The process of occupational

---

[1] *Occupational therapists* are responsible for all aspects of occupational therapy service delivery and are accountable for the safety and effectiveness of the occupational therapy service delivery process. *Occupational therapy assistants* deliver occupational therapy services under the supervision of and in partnership with occupational therapists (AOTA, 2009). When the term *occupational therapy practitioner* is used in this document, it refers to both occupational therapists and occupational therapy assistants (AOTA, 2006).

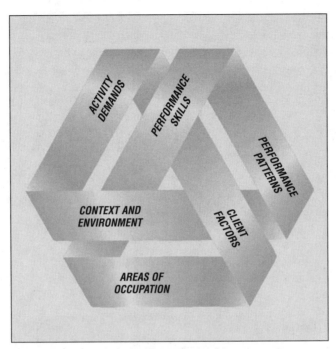

Figure 1. Occupational therapy's domain. Supporting health and participation in life through engagement in occupation.

Note. Mobius originally designed by Mark Dow. Used with permission.

Source: American Occupational Therapy Association. (2008). Occupational therapy practice framework: Domain and process (2nd ed., p. 627). *American Journal of Occupational Therapy, 62,* 625–683. Used with permission.

AREAS OF OCCUPATION	CLIENT FACTORS	PERFORMANCE SKILLS	PERFORMANCE PATTERNS	CONTEXT AND ENVIRONMENT	ACTIVITY DEMANDS
Activities of Daily Living (ADL)* Instrumental Activities of Daily Living (IADL) Rest and Sleep Education Work Play Leisure Social Participation? *Also referred to as *basic activities of daily living (BADL)* or *personal activities of daily living (PADL)*.	Values, Beliefs, and Spirituality Body Functions Body Structures	Sensory Perceptual Skills Motor and Praxis Skills Emotional Regulation Skills Cognitive Skills Communication and Social Skills	Habits Routines Roles Rituals	Cultural Personal Physical Social Temporal Virtual	Objects Used and Their Properties Space Demands Social Demands Sequencing and Timing Required Actions Required Body Functions Required Body Structures

Figure 2. Aspects of occupational therapy's domain.

Source: American Occupational Therapy Association. (2008). Occupational therapy practice framework: Domain and process (2nd ed., p. 628). *American Journal of Occupational Therapy, 62,* 625–683. Used with permission.

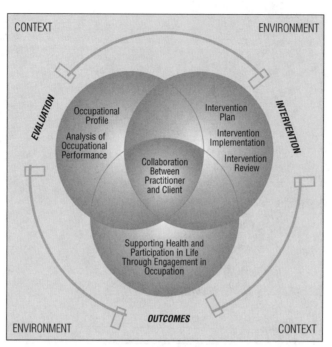

Figure 3. Occupational therapy's process. Collaboration between the practitioner and the client is central to the interactive nature of service delivery.

Source: American Occupational Therapy Association. (2008). Occupational therapy practice framework: Domain and process (2nd ed., p. 627). *American Journal of Occupational Therapy, 62,* 625–683. Used with permission.

therapy service delivery begins with the *occupational profile*, an assessment of the client's occupational needs, problems, and concerns, and the *analysis of occupational performance*, which includes the skills, patterns, contexts and environments, activity demands, and client factors that contribute to or impede the client's satisfaction with his or her ability to engage in valued daily life activities. Therapists then plan and implement intervention using a variety of approaches and methods in which occupation is both the mean and end (Trombly, 1995). Occupational therapists continually assess the effectiveness of the intervention they provide and the client's progress toward targeted outcomes. The *intervention review* informs decisions to continue or discontinue intervention and to make referrals to other agencies or professionals. Therapists select outcome measures that are valid, reliable, and appropriately sensitive to the client's occupational performance, adaptation, health and wellness, prevention, quality of life, role competence, self-advocacy, and occupational justice.

■ ■ ■

Introduction

Historical Aspects

Autism is a neurodevelopmental disorder with onset prior to age 3 characterized by qualitative impairments in social interactions and communication skills, along with a restricted, repetitive and stereotyped pattern of behavior, interests, and activities (American Psychiatric Association [APA], 2001; World Health Organization [WHO], 1994). It is identified in the *Diagnostic and Statistical Manual of Mental Disorders, 4th Edition Text Revision* (*DSM-IV-TR;* APA, 2001) as one of the five pervasive developmental disorders: autism, pervasive developmental disorder not otherwise specified (PDD–NOS), Asperger syndrome, childhood disintegrative disorder, and Rett syndrome. All of these conditions are characterized by varying degrees of difficulty in communication skills; social interactions; and restricted, repetitive, and stereotyped patterns of behavior.

The terms *autism* and *autistic* stem from the Greek word *autos*, meaning *self*. Swiss psychiatrist Eugen Bleuler (1911) first used "autism" to describe the social withdrawal of adults with schizophrenia. Later, in 1943, Dr. Leo Kanner (1943) first described autism as it is currently understood, basing his discovery on 11 children he observed between 1938 and 1943 who appeared to share a number of common characteristics that he suggested formed a "unique 'syndrome' not heretofore reported" (p. 242). His paper characterized the children as possessing an "extreme autistic aloneness" from early in life. The following year, Hans Asperger (1944) published, in German, "Autistic Psychopathy in Childhood." The paper presented a case study of several children whom he described as examples of "a particularly interesting and highly recognizable type of child" (p. 76). Asperger's *autistic psychopathy* description is far wider than Kanner's, including cases demonstrating severe organic damage and those bordering on normalcy. Both Kanner and Asperger believed that the chil-dren experienced a fundamental disturbance that gave rise to additional characteristic problems. They both chose the word *autism* to characterize the nature of this underlying disturbance, that is, the inability to sustain ongoing relationships with people.

During the 1940s, 1950s, and 1960s, the medical community considered children with autism to be schizophrenic. In fact, "infantile autism" was listed as a form of schizophrenia in the *International Statistical Classification of Diseases and Related Health Problems* (*ICD;* WHO, 1980). It was thought that the children experienced emotional disturbances resulting from early attachment experiences. Bruno Bettelheim (1967) wrote about three children in *The Empty Fortress*. He called them autistic and claimed that their disorder was due to the coldness of their mothers (i.e., "refrigerator parents"), and as a result, he completely disengaged the parents from the children's therapy. This lack of understanding of the disorder led many parents to believe that they were at fault for their child's condition.

Through the late 1960s and 1970s, research studies began to delineate autism as a distinct disorder with a possible neurological basis associated with developmental conditions and mental retardation. This new research focus challenged the notion that autism was an early manifestation of schizophrenia and debunked the theory of refrigerator parents. With this increased awareness and clarity in diagnostic symptomology, autism was officially recognized as a developmental disorder in the 3rd Edition of the *DSM* (APA, 1980). Within this classification, infantile autism was included in a new class of disorder, the pervasive developmental disorders (PDD). Significant changes were made to the autism diagnosis with the revision of *DSM-III* to *DSM-III-R* (APA, 1987). Although PDD was retained as the broad class to which autism was assigned, the term "infantile" was dropped to reflect the recognition that the symptoms of autism continue into childhood. This also emphasized the need for a more developmental approach to establishing and treating individuals with the diagnosis. Additionally, a new subthreshold category of PDD–NOS was added. With *DSM-III-R,* 16 diagnostic criteria were established, of which children were required to present with 8 to receive a diagnosis of autism. Around the same time, Wing (1981) introduced the term *Asperger syndrome* to reflect a higher-functioning model of Kanner's early autism.

Research efforts continued to clarify diagnostic criteria and broaden the category. With *DSM-IV* (APA, 1994), clearer criteria for autism and PDD–NOS were presented to minimize overidentification. Additionally, Asperger syndrome was included as a distinct disorder for the first time. This inclusion again broadened the PDD category. In the same decade, two additional related changes occurred. First, with the reauthorization of the Individuals with Disabilities Education Act (IDEA) in 1990, autism was recognized as an eligible condition to qualify for special education services. Second, the *ICD-10* (WHO, 1994) was revised to improve the consistency in diagnostic criteria with the *DSM*. With the *DSM-IV-TR* (APA, 2001), diagnostic criteria for autism and Asperger syndrome were unchanged, although the criteria for PDD–NOS was revised in an attempt to improve the clarity of the diagnostic considerations.

Today, autism remains one of the disorders within the PDD umbrella. The conditions within PDD are characterized by differing degrees of difficulty in communication skills; social interactions; and restricted, repetitive, and stereotyped patterns of behavior. The term *pervasive developmental disorder* was adopted to provide a formal diagnosis for individuals who shared the essential deficits associated with autism but did not meet the full diagnostic criteria for autism. The intent was to emphasize the pervasiveness of the impairments in many aspects of daily life while allowing for differentiation from those with general mental retardation. Therefore, PDDs are often described as *spectrum disorders,* with autism as the prototype, and other disorders with decreasing severity and fewer domains of devel-

opment affected (Lord & Risi, 2000). At present, the range of disorders is referred to as the *autism spectrum disorders (ASDs)* rather than the PDDs. This shift in terminology reflects better awareness by researchers and clinicians that services often appropriate for individuals with autism are suitable for individuals with an ASD (Johnson, Myers, & Council on Children With Disabilities, 2007; Lord & Risi, 2000). It also reflects general agreement that individuals with lesser impairments should also be considered part of the spectrum (i.e., the ASD spectrum ranges from severe autism to mild autism to Asperger syndrome). If a child presents with symptoms of either of these disorders but does not meet the specific criteria for either, the diagnosis *pervasive developmental disorder–not otherwise specified* (PDD–NOS) is used. Rett syndrome and childhood disintegrative disorder are very severe, rare forms of ASDs and are not included in this review. Diagnostic criteria for the types of ASD are summarized in Table 1. This Practice Guideline will focus on autism, PDD–NOS, and Asperger syndrome.

Diagnostic criteria for the disorders on the autism spectrum are defined by those developmental domains involved (i.e., social, language, behavior) and the severity of the presenting deficits (APA, 2001). A diagnosis of autism requires onset prior to age 3, with impairments of differing degrees noted in communication and social domains, along with restricted, repetitive, and stereotyped patterns of behavior. In Asperger syndrome, impairments are noted within the social and behavioral domains, while communication milestones for onset and development of language are generally appropriate. PDD–NOS encompasses cases in which the individual exhibits marked impairment in reciprocal social interaction in either verbal and nonverbal communication skills or with stereotyped behavior patterns or interest, but full criteria are not met for any of the other PDDs. As an example, a child may present and not meet full criteria for autism because of a later onset age, atypical symptoms, subthreshold symptoms, or all of these (APA, 2001).

One challenging aspect in recognizing that a child has an ASD is the significant variability in characteristics and range of severity that a child may exhibit. Even

Table 1. Pervasive Developmental Disorders (PDDs)

Autistic Disorder (299.00/299.00)	• Qualitative impairments in social interaction • Qualitative impairments in communication • Restricted, repetitive, and stereotyped pattern of behaviors, interests, and activities • Onset prior to 3 years

PDD–NOS or Atypical Autism (299.80/299.80)	• Severe or pervasive impairment in: Reciprocal social interaction or verbal and nonverbal communication or stereotyped behaviors, interests, and activities
	• Criteria are not met for
	  • Another PDD
	  • Schizophrenia
	  • Schizotypal Personality Disorder
	  • Avoidant Personality Disorder.

Asperger Syndrome (299.80/299.80)	• Qualitative impairments in social interaction • Restricted, repetitive, and stereotyped pattern of behaviors, interests, and activities • No cognitive impairment • Criteria for qualitative impairments in communication are not met

Childhood Disintegrative Disorder (299.10/299.10)	• Apparently normal development for first 2 years in areas of play, communication, social relations, and adaptive behavior
	• Loss of previously acquired skills by 10 years in at least two of the following:
	  • Expressive or receptive communication
	  • Social skills or adaptive behavior
	  • Bowel or bladder control
	  • Play
	  • Motor skills.
	• Abnormalities of functioning in two of the three core deficit areas of autism

Rett Disorder (299.80/330.80)	• Normal development for first 5 months • Deceleration of head growth (5–48 months) • Loss of purposeful hand skills and development of stereotyped movements • Loss of social engagement • Severely impaired expressive and receptive language development • Poor coordination and psychomotor retardation

Note. Diagnostic codes following labels indicate *DSM-IV-TR* (APA, 2001)/*International Classification of Diseases-9th Edition-Clinical Modification* (*ICD-9-CM*; American Medical Association, 2008).

within the same diagnosis, presentation will vary from one child to the next, with no two children presenting with the same symptoms. Further, in addition to severity, the spectrum is differentiated by age of onset and comorbid delay. For example, a child may meet criteria for Asperger syndrome because he or she does not meet autism diagnostic criteria for onset prior to age 3 and has no cognitive or language delay. Another child also diagnosed with Asperger syndrome, however, may present prior to age 3 with significant social deficits and a pattern of restricted interests and activities but may not have sufficient language deficits to establish an autism diagnosis. As discussed above, the ASDs have overlapping core deficits and imprecise end points for each diagnosis. Further, presentation of the disorder in the same child will also change over time, as summarized in Table 2.

In addition to the core diagnostic social, communication, and repetitive behavior features of autism, motor skill delays and aberrant sensory responding also have been widely reported in the literature describing children and adolescents with an ASD. Functional limitations in these areas are often the focus of intervention services from occupational therapy practitioners. Appendix A provides a review of motor performance and sensory processing findings reported in the literature.

Table 2. Developmental Presentation of the ASDs Through Adolescence

Age	Social	Communication	Behavior
Toddler/ Preschool	■ Lack of use of eye contact; looks through people ■ Decreased awareness of others ■ Lack of joint attention or shared enjoyment ■ Unable to read facial expressions and not sensitive to the feelings of others ■ Limited initiation and interaction with others ■ Poor imitation	■ Delayed verbal language ■ Impaired nonverbal communication (e.g., eye gaze, pointing, gestures) ■ Communicative attempts limited to protesting and requesting only ■ Echolalic speech ■ Lack of imaginative and pretend play ■ Regression in language ■ Nonresponsive to language	■ Repetitive interests (e.g., lines up toys, watches only certain parts of movies, stuck on one show or one character from a show) ■ Difficulty with transitioning between tasks or activities ■ Motor stereotypes (e.g., hand or finger mannerisms, toe walking) ■ Unusual responding to sensory input
School	■ Difficulty relating to both adults and peers ■ Inability to engage in cooperative play with peers ■ Unable to understand or follow rules of a classroom ■ Decreased awareness of social norms during interaction (e.g., touch, eye gaze/contact, personal space)	■ Abnormal prosody of speech ■ Persistent echolalia ■ Developed verbal language, although limited use for social purposes ■ Errors with pronoun use	■ Routine-based behavior; insistence on sameness ■ Difficulty with cognitive flexibility and generalization of skills across environments ■ Failure to see the gestalt (i.e., hyperfocus on one detail)
Adolescence	■ Poor social judgment ■ Anxious in social situations ■ Continued lack of awareness of social norms during interaction ■ Inability to learn group rules ■ Difficulty with establishing and maintaining peer relationships, although greater ease with adults	■ Prosody abnormalities persist ■ Pragmatic (social use) language deficits ■ Concrete interpretation of language and a lack of understanding of sarcasm or metaphors ■ Inability to coordinate nonverbal (e.g., eye contact, body proximity) with language	■ Deficits with executive functions leading to decreased simultaneous processing ■ Some have a refinement of their special interest and develop a more discrete special interest ■ Routine-based behavior; insistence on sameness

Note. ASDs = autism spectrum disorders.

Prevalence

Appreciating that these historical changes in diagnostic criteria and categories have significant implications for understanding prevalence, or the proportion of the population with ASDs, the Centers for Disease Control and Prevention (CDC, 2007a, 2007b) has tracked the ASD prevalence since 2000, utilizing multisite data collection. In February 2007, the CDC reported initial findings of the surveillance program involving 14 sites for the 2000 and 2002 time periods, with ASD rates ranging from 1 in 303 to 1 in 94 children. Based on these initial data, the CDC estimates an average ASD rate of 1 in 150, or 6.6 in 1,000 children. A similar ASD prevalence rate of 1 in 166 children has been reported in recent epidemiologic studies (Fombonne, 2003a, 2003b). These epidemiologic studies have reported a 4:1 male-to-female ratio (Fombonne, 2003a). This ratio, however,

appears to vary by intelligence level, with the highest male-to-female ratios reported in individuals functioning in the normal range on cognitive assessment, and the lowest ratios found in individuals with autism and profound mental retardation (Lord, Schopler, & Revicki, 1982; McLennan, Lord, & Schopler, 1993; Volkmar, Szatmari, & Sparrow, 1993).

Consistently, national incidence studies report ASDs to be on the increase, with much debate in the field as to potential reasons (Prior, 2003; Rutter, 2005; Wing & Potter, 2002). And while current studies reflect a tenfold increase across ASDs from studies published a decade ago, the rise appears to be the greatest in those with nonverbal IQs in the normal range (Rutter, 2005). This implies broadening of the diagnostic criteria and therefore likely reflects the full ASD spectrum with inclusion of PDD–NOS and Asperger syndrome, as opposed to autism in isolation. Because of this, it has been questioned whether the incidence of autism is increasing or whether this increase reflects changes in diagnosis procedures and criteria. Following the inclusion of autism as a diagnosis making children eligible for school-based services (IDEA, 1990), the U.S. Department of Education (1999) reported a 172.86% increase in the number of children ages 6–21 years served from 1988–1989 through 1997–1998. Further, in a report of the U.S. Government Accountability Office (2005) reporting on special education services of individuals with autism, a 500% increase in the number of children with autism served under IDEA was reported over the past decade. Prior to the IDEA reauthorization, many of these children were likely served under emotional–behavior disorder, developmental delay, learning disability, or speech impairment distinctions. However, with autism available as a distinct condition qualifying a child for service provision, many individualized educational programs may have been changed in this period to accurately reflect the eligibility diagnosis.

Additionally, reports of increasing numbers of children with ASDs also have heightened public awareness of the disorder and led to increased efforts to identify possible sources of etiology. Currently, no single known or definitive cause has been identified. There is, however, universal agreement that the ASDs are biologically based neurodevelopmental disorders that are genetically mediated (Bailey, Phillips, & Rutter, 1996; Buxbaum, 2005; Veenstra-Vanderweele, Christian, & Cook, 2004). ASDs are believed to be related to changes in regional structural and functional neural networks of the brain, likely based in abnormal regulation of multiple genetic processes (DiCicco-Bloom et al., 2006; Johnson et al., 2007; Kabot, Masi, & Segal, 2003; Ozonoff, Goodlin-Jones, & Solomon, 2005). In addition, unidentified factors within the prenatal and postnatal environments may trigger the onset of symptoms. As such, the etiology is likely multifactorial (Filipek et al., 2000; Veenstra-Vanderweele et al., 2004). It is beyond the scope of this guideline to review these neurological and genetic factors; interested readers should consult more recent in-depth reviews (Bauman & Kemper, 2004; DiCicco-Bloom et al., 2006).

Given the neurobiologic and genetic basis of the ASDs, comorbid conditions are often associated with the disorders. In medicine and in psychiatry, comorbidity describes the effect of diseases an individual patient might have other than the primary disease of interest. From a medical perspective, many individuals with an ASD develop seizures in early childhood or during a second peak of onset, with first occurrence of seizures during adolescence (Volkmar, 2000). As many as 35% of individuals with autism may develop seizures by adulthood (Filipek et al., 2000). Autism has also been associated with Fragile X syndrome, the most common known genetic cause of mental retardation. The prevalence of Fragile X is between 1/3,500 and 1/9,000 in males, and the prevalence of autism among individuals with Fragile X is estimated at 25%–33% (Bailey et al., 1998; Rogers, Wehner, & Hagerman, 2001). Conversely, the prevalence of Fragile X in individuals with autism was recently estimated at 2.1% (Kielinen, Rantala, Timonen, Linna, & Moilanen, 2004). Associations also have been reported between autism and tuberous sclerosis, a neurocutaneous autosomal dominant disorder that causes abnormal tissue growth in the brain. The prevalence of autism in tuberous sclerosis is estimated from 16% to over 65%, and, conversely, the prevalence of tuberous sclerosis in autism is estimated at 0%–4% and perhaps as high as 8%–14% among the subgroup of autistic individuals with a seizure disorder (Smalley, 1998; Wong, 2006).

Individuals with an ASD have increased rates of psychiatric disorders, such as anxiety disorders, depression, and obsessive behavior (Ghaziuddin, Ghaziuddin, & Greden, 2002; Matson & Nebel-Schwalm, 2007). Additionally, increased prevalence of attention deficit disorders has been reported (Reiersen & Todd, 2008; Sturm, Fernell, & Gilberg, 2004) in children with an ASD.

When considered together, the epidemiologic data indicate that as many as 1.5 million Americans today have an ASD (Autism Society of America [ASA], 2008). This represents a large population of individuals who are in need of ongoing services, some of which will be provided by occupational therapy practitioners. The remainder of this guideline focuses on the occupational therapy process for individuals with an ASD.

Occupational Therapy Process for Individuals With an ASD

The process of occupational therapy services for individuals with ASDs includes evaluation and intervention focused on salient outcomes that include but are not limited to the individual's occupational performance, adaptation, health and wellness, participation in the community, quality of life, role competence, self-advocacy, and occupational justice (AOTA, 2008b). Services are initiated when an individual client's functional difficulties impede engagement in occupations and participation in everyday life activities. The evaluation includes gathering, interpreting, and synthesizing information relevant to the client's past and current occupational engagement and performance as well as desired future participation, and specific evaluation of current occupational performance. Occupational therapy intervention is individually designed and is aimed at improving the client's desired and expected occupational engagement and participation through implementation of interventions and procedures directed at the client, the activity, and the environment. When developing an intervention, occupational therapy practitioners always consider the dynamic nature of the context in which the client is expected to perform. The occupational therapy process also includes monitoring the client's response to the intervention, reevaluating and modifying the intervention plan, and measuring intervention success through outcomes that are relevant and meaningful to the individual The occupational therapy process is holistic and client- and family-centered, with consideration for the dynamic interaction of the individual and the internal neurophysiological and external physical, social, and cultural contexts of function. Occupational therapy is fluid, dynamic, and interactive, using engagement in occupations as both the method and desired outcome of the process.

Referral: Diagnostic vs. Intervention Planning Assessment

A referral initiated by a parent/caregiver, physician, or school personnel usually begins the occupational therapy process. Occupational therapy services are requested for individuals with an ASD when functional performance limitations are present (e.g., in movement, sensory processing, or adaptive behavior). The reason for referral in many cases is dependent on the setting in which the practitioner functions (Nelson, 1982). While in almost all cases the evaluation is ultimately requested to document the strengths and weaknesses of an individual for appropriate program planning, correctly identifying the reason for referral will help the practitioner define his or her role and assure specialized referral questions are answered.

Because diagnosis is best made by having professionals from various disciplines assess development in many areas (Filipek et al., 1999, 2000; Ozonoff et al., 2005; Stone & Ousley, 1996), an occupational therapist will likely be a member of a multidisciplinary team contributing to the diagnostic evaluation. Specific practice parameters for the diagnostic assessment of ASDs have been published by the American Academy of Neurology (AAN; Filipek et al., 2000), the American Academy of Child and Adolescent Psychiatry (AACAP; Volkmar, Cook, Pomeroy, Realmuto, & Tanguay, 1999), the American Pediatric Association (APA; Johnson et al., 2007), and a consensus panel with representation from multiple professional societies, including AOTA (Filipek et al., 1999). These parameters describe two levels of diagnostic assessment. The first level is screening as part of routine developmental monitoring. The second level, for those who fail the screening, involves a multidisciplinary assessment by a variety of clinicians with experience working with individuals with an ASD.

During a multidisciplinary team evaluation, the occupational therapist will have a defined role. For example, the focus may be on addressing sensorimotor aspects of development that may be contributing to the child's developmental presentation (Filipek et al., 2000; Volkmar et al., 1999). In this situation, the focus of the occupational therapy assessment might be on sensory processing (including praxis) and occupational performance rather than the evaluation of motor milestones. Additionally, fostering a greater understanding in other team members of the influence of a sensory processing disorder on behavior and performance abilities may be critical for differential diagnosis. For example, during an interdisciplinary assessment of a very driven and active toddler, the child is found to have cognitive, motor, and communication delays. When discussing potential diagnoses for the child, much of the discussion by the team members revolves around the impact of the child's impulsivity and activity level on social communication development and overall task performance. These difficulties with behavioral regulation may relate to the child's cognitive delays, early indications of a coexisting attention deficit or anxiety disorder, or a sensory processing disorder. When multidisciplinary team members collaborate to define specific features of the diagnosis, the most appropriate intervention program can be developed.

In many cases, the purpose of the diagnostic evaluation process not only will be establishing or ruling out a diagnosis but also comprehensively assessing specific skill areas for individualized intervention planning. In comprehensive evaluations, team members often have well-defined roles and expectations because the individual skill areas assessed are interrelated with the skills assessed by other team members. Further, professionals of different disciplines approach assessment using different frames of reference and, as a result, may have different interpretations of observations made during the evaluation. Therefore, findings need to be integrated to develop a coherent intervention plan. This conceptual integration may provide a clearer understanding of the presentation of the individual with an ASD and lead to appropriate intervention. For example, a psychologist functioning independently and working from a strict behavioral frame of reference may interpret a self-stimulatory behavior or stereotypy as a behavior to be extinguished. However, that stereotypy, when analyzed by an occupational therapist, may be interpreted as a self-regulatory mechanism to control behavior in a classroom setting. The team together develops a program from an integrated interpretation with the overriding goal of reducing the behavior. The team decides to provide the child with additional supports in the classroom to assist with self-regulation, along with a measurement system to monitor the behavior.

Whether a referral is made for diagnostic or treatment planning purposes, the occupational therapy practitioner likely will be asked to document the strengths and weaknesses of an individual. Having the roles of each discipline clearly defined ensures that specialized areas are addressed and all referral questions are answered. Sharing of referral questions and teaming with the other professionals and the family of the individual with an ASD allows for appropriate diagnosis, program planning, and intervention development.

Evaluation

Occupational Profile

Given the social communication difficulties experienced by an individual with an ASD, the evaluation process usually begins with the occupational profile as reported by the parents of the child. This process varies according to the environment and context in which services will be provided but is generally completed in the initial session. During ongoing service provision, this information may be collected over several sessions as part of the therapeutic process.

The occupational profile identifies the child's occupational history and current occupations in various contexts and discusses typical routines and the child's interests and motivations. Additionally, the profile explores problematic daily routines. The current social supports (i.e., family and friend membership, peer relationships, community resources, intervention programs) are identified to guide information gathering related to functioning and engagement in childhood occupations. The profile also includes concerns, questions, and priorities. Interviewing the family using the Canadian Occupational Performance Measure (COPM; Law et al., 2005) may assist this process. Additionally, instruments developed for use with children and appropriate for children with disabilities, such as the Perceived Efficacy and Goal Setting System (PEGS; Missiuna, Pollock, & Law, 2004) and Children's Assessment of Participation and Enjoyment and Preferences for Activities of Children (CAPE/PAC; King et al., 2005), may be administered. Both instruments allow for parent or teacher assistance to complete the assessment items and involve use of pictures to identify activity preferences for common daily living and school tasks. The nonverbal and highly visual nature of these assessment tools make them desirable for use with this group of children, especially higher functioning individuals with some language.

Information gathered in the occupational profile is used to guide the family-centered evaluation and intervention process. Using this information, the occupational therapist can identify the strengths and limitations of the child and family and, in turn, can identify relevant evaluation methods to assess the underlying components of the identified impairments. In collaboration with the team, the evaluation findings are used to establish goals and guide intervention planning. The child with autism may not be able to directly identify intervention priorities given the social and communication deficits; however, use of the PEGS or CAPE/PAC in conjunction with structured observation of play and behavior will allow the practitioner to integrate similar components of these activities and provide insight into the child's interests, impairments, and overall functioning.

Evaluation Considerations

When providing services to individuals with an ASD, occupational therapy practitioners work with families and a variety of professionals (e.g., educators, speech–language pathologists, behavior therapists) and paraprofessionals (e.g., instructional assistants, bus drivers, lunchroom personnel) in many settings. Factors that influence the evaluation process are briefly discussed in the following section.

Setting and context considerations. Occupational therapists may evaluate children in their home, school, diagnostic center, residential center, and/or community. This context in which the occupational therapist provides service influences the evaluation process. For example, a school-based therapist will likely evaluate participation in traditional school occupations relevant to academic and nonacademic curriculum goals, whereas an occupational therapist in a residential center may focus on activities of daily living (ADLs) and instrumental activities of daily living (IADLs). On a diagnostic evaluation team, in addition to evaluating functional aspects of development, the occupational therapist generally provides relevant observations regarding social and play skill development.

Further, the symptoms of autism and their impact on participation may vary across environments, so evaluating behaviors within various settings is also important. Experts have noted that structured observation is most useful to the diagnostic and intervention planning process, and is most accurate when accomplished within the child's natural settings (Kientz & Dunn, 1997; Kientz & Miller, 1999; Rutter & Schopler, 1988; Watson & Marcus, 1988). Analysis of performance in the natural setting allows for observation of the child's typical behavior and performance in functional everyday activities that are familiar parts of the child's daily routine. Because children with an ASD often have difficulty transitioning to new surroundings and working with new people, conducting evaluation activities in their natural environments can reduce the effects that a new setting might have on the child's behavior and performance. Therefore, observation in multiple settings can provide significant information diagnosis. In this case, it is felt that use of standardized assessments developed for the sole purpose of identifying the presence and severity of an ASD (e.g., Autism Diagnostic Interview–Revised [Lord, Rutter, & LeCouteur, 1994], Autism Diagnostic Observation Schedule [Lord, Rutter, DiLavore, & Risi, 2002]) always should be used.

Multiple measures are used in assessment. Whether using standardized or nonstandardized instruments, the focus of the assessment process should be on obtaining information on the individual's occupational performance. A variety of strategies, including direct assessment, naturalistic observation, and structured interview (Filipek et al., 1999; Ozonoff et al., 2005; Rutter & Schopler, 1988), should be used to maximize information-gathering efforts. When using direct assessment, adaptations to the typical testing situation, environment, and/or materials likely will be necessary to obtain the most accurate measure and ensure optimal performance of the individual (Filipek et al., 1999, 2000; Schopler et al., 1980). Additional visits may be necessary for the child to adapt to the environment and/or the evaluator and to transition into the process of testing (Filipek et al., 1999). Verbal directions may be too difficult for the child to comprehend, so the evaluator may need to adapt the directions using simple (e.g., one word) or nonverbal means (e.g., gesture, model, present a picture; Schopler et al., 1980). For example, while evaluating dressing, a therapist in a residential setting places a shoe on the floor next to the adolescent being evaluated and directs him to "Put your shoe on." If he does not understand the directive, he may pick up the shoe and play with the strings or do nothing with the shoe and leave the table. When the directive is simplified by saying only "On" and pairing it with pointing toward the shoe, he then may put on the shoe. In simplifying the command, the targeted assessment of dressing was achieved while also gathering information on the child's receptive-language abilities and learning style that can be used to guide the rest of the evaluation process.

In another example, a child may not be able to sit in a chair to respond to fine and visual–motor items presented at a table. If the child appears to need more sensory input as a means of regulating his behavior, presenting items while he is seated on a moving system (e.g., platform swing, large equilibrium board) may allow for better arousal regulation and task performance.

In making the above adaptations, standard scores, if used, must be qualified in the written report. An adapted testing process increases the chances that the results accurately represent the child's unique abilities while also providing information on areas of relative weakness. Because successful learning is based on utilizing a child's strong skills to foster growth in areas of weakness, accurately defining a child's unique strengths and limitations is the first step in assuring appropriate differential diagnosis, program planning, and intervention development.

Play as an evaluation method. Play is a child's main occupation and therefore requires special attention in a child with ASD in the evaluation. Unfortunately, play often is evaluated in this vein: What the child is *not* doing while playing instead of *how* the child plays and *what* motivates him or her in play. Therefore, observations of play not only should describe a child's level of play skills but also take into account the qualitative aspects of the play for future use in interactions with the child. Formal assessment of play will be discussed later in this evaluation section. Here, play will be discussed as an evaluation method and specifically as a way to adapt testing.

Play can be a powerful evaluation method because it provides insight into a child's social, motor, cognitive, and sensory processing skills. Additionally, play often becomes the framework from which other areas are evaluated. From the onset of a direct assessment, a therapist observes the child's sensorimotor, social, adaptive, and communication behavior in play. These observations of play can be used to guide clinical decision making for evaluation methods and adaptation of standard measures, as well as allow the therapist to better understand a child's motivation to participate in testing and his or her apparent learning style. For example, when a therapist at a diagnostic center goes to the waiting room to bring a child and his family into the testing areas for an evaluation, she notes that the child is walking back and forth along a window, vocalizing, and not interacting with the other children in the waiting area. When his name is called, the child does not respond; when the child sees his parents stand and approach the therapist, he briefly looks at his parents before going back to walking along the window. His parents ask him to come, but he does not respond. However, when they put out their hands and start walking toward the clinic, the child runs after them.

As they walk to the clinic, the therapist notes the child vocalizing in delayed echolalia, a script from SpongeBob SquarePants® cartoons. From these observations, the therapist infers that the child likes movement, tends to respond better to visual information than verbal, and that he has some interest and knowledge of SpongeBob SquarePants. In turn, these factors can be used to make decisions about testing methods and ways to structure the play aspects of assessment to maximize performance. In this case, the therapist likely will maximize the performance of and interaction with the child by utilizing visual supports for structure and direction, as well as incorporating movement-based play. Additionally, tasks can be adapted to a SpongeBob SquarePants theme (e.g., stacking and constructional praxis items can be adapted to making "crabby patties"; drawing of shapes in imitation can be to make a picture of SpongeBob SquarePants).

The above example also illustrates how some observations of a child in play reflect the child's restricted or repetitive play repertoire and therefore can become a part of the evaluation methods by creating activities or adapting current activities to make them naturally reinforcing. As another example, when evaluating an older, higher-functioning child at school, the therapist notices that the child often makes references to different game shows. Knowing this allows the therapist to structure the whole evaluation as a game show. Individual tasks on a standardized motor measure can be made into timed challenges, and writing tasks can be structured so the child is answering Final Jeopardy!® questions.

Given the significant impact this type of structuring of play can have on the overall success of the process, information about the child's motivations also may be gathered formally. As such, a reinforcer assessment may be used to gather this information prior to the evaluation or as part of the occupational profile. A reinforcer assessment defines the activities in which the child most often engages, along with their food, toy, video, and television preferences. This information can be collected formally as a checklist as seen in Appendix B or done through an interview during the occupational profile.

Information gleaned from the reinforcer assessment can be used to structure or adapt activities to facilitate increased participation from the child. For example, an occupational therapist sets up an obstacle course to evaluate motor skill; however, the child resists participating in the activity. The therapist recalls that during discussions with the parents while conducting the occupational profile, they indicated that the child loves watching Dora the Explorer® and that he often has immediate and delayed echolalia of the song that the Map® sings in the cartoon. Knowing this information, the therapist sings the song and moves through the obstacle course. After observing the first time, the child joins in as the song is restarted.

In another example, a child engages in primarily solitary play lining up blocks. He is resistant to a therapist's attempt to join in the play and transition his lining up to a block-stacking activity. He reportedly is tactilely hypersensitive and becomes upset when someone tries to use hand-over-hand assistance. Instead, knowing the child likes Winnie the Pooh® and other Pooh characters, the therapist brings out a Pooh puppet to stack the blocks and a bouncing Tigger® toy to knock them over. Presenting the blocks alongside the child while he is in free play may elicit some spontaneous interaction so that a directive may be given or a task can be modeled. When stacking two blocks, the bouncing Tigger knocks them down to immediately reinforce the successful performance and facilitate continued interaction. Taking the time to structure these observations can be instrumental in facilitating the child's engagement in the evaluation process.

ment, with special attention directed to the types of toys and the nature of the interaction with these toys. Interactions may be repetitive, and the child may show an intense attachment and/or prolonged play with a certain object or objects. Conversely, the child may have a short attention span and shift his attention frequently from toy to toy. The therapist should also note the extent to which the child draws others into his play.

Identifying these factors provides the practitioner insight into functional play levels and allows him or her to draw upon common features that can be used in intervention. For example, a child spends a significant amount of time during an evaluation in independent play with cars. His play with the cars is largely repetitive in nature, as he lines them up, sorts by color, or engages in container play (repetitively filling a box and then dumping it out). He also frequently closely visually inspects the cars with peripheral vision when they are lined up, dropped in the box, or turned over and the wheels spun. When considered together, these observations provide insight regarding the child's developmental level for play that includes container play and sorting and highlights the child's preference for structured play. The interest in colors and presence of unusual visual inspection provide guidance for the components of future activities that could be used to expand play. Because the child sort colors accurately, color sorting could be used to teach the child to count with one-to-one correspondence.

Therapists should also document stereotypies. The presence, frequency, and/or triggers of repetitive motor stereotypies, unusual body posturing, object stereotypies, self-injurious behaviors, and vocal stereotypies are noted through observation or by report of caregivers. Hand flapping, finger mannerisms, toe walking, head banging, and body rocking have been specifically reported as examples of stereotypies common to people with an ASD. Interpretation of the stereotypies will determine the extent to which they interfere with the individual's social or task engagement or are a barrier to new skill acquisition.

Therapists should also document structured observations of externalizing behaviors exhibited during structured play and evaluation. The therapists should consider the child's ability to manage and express emotions, control impulses, and delay gratification within and between tasks. Further, qualitative differences may be noted in these behaviors, on the basis of whether the play is structured or unstructured. Additionally, as the demands of tasks change, the therapist observes the child's frustration tolerance/anger management and coping skills. These observations can be considered in relation to other play observations to define potential antecedents of problematic behaviors and social–emotional or social communication impairments that may limit the child's social participation.

Participation in areas of occupation. Individuals diagnosed with an ASD often have limitations in performance in one or more areas of occupation. Depending on the age of the individual being assessed, play performance, school occupations, adaptive behavior, and ADLs may be evaluated. However, in addition to these everyday occupations, it is important to note that children with autism frequently engage in unusual occupations related to their restricted pattern of behavior that may be viewed as irrelevant to others (Spitzer, 2003a, 2003b, 2004, 2008). Although the child's action may not appear purposeful, it is probable that child has specific intent in his or her actions. Therefore, observations of a child's occupational behavior within play, school, and adaptive domains need to be framed from a broad occupational perspective to understand the unique value or meaning to the child (Spitzer, 2003a, 2003b, 2004).

Play. Play is the main activity of childhood and, as a result, influences the development of motor, social communication, cognitive, and self-care domains. Children with an ASD often have a limited play repertoire, so play needs special attention as part of the evaluation (APA, 2001; Filipek et al., 1999; Kientz & Miller-Kuhaneck, 2001; Stone, Lemanek, Fishel, Fernandez, & Altemeier, 1990). Play deficits, including delayed onset and a limited play repertoire, are well documented and are hallmark diagnostic features within social and repetitive behavior categories of symptoms (Filipek et al., 1999, 2000; Stone et al., 1990; Wainwright & Fein, 1996). Assessment of play most often is accomplished through structured clinical observations (see Table 4)

Table 4. Play Observations

Area	Observations/Questions
Social Communication	▪ What means of communication are used in play (e.g., proximity, eye contact, eye gaze, social referencing, joint attention, handing objects, using others' hand as a tool, gestures, echolalic speech, spontaneous speech)? ▪ What communicative functions does the child express (e.g., request, protest, comment, interaction, choice making)? ▪ Do the child's communicative functions and means differ in spontaneous vs. structured play, or with adults vs. peers? ▪ Does the child initiate play or only respond? ▪ What is the level of social interaction (e.g., does the child watch peers, or does he or she engage in solitary, parallel, or cooperative play)? ▪ How does the child react to other children entering his or her play? ▪ Does the child rely on adult interaction and supervision to guide his or her play? ▪ Does the child take turns? ▪ Can the child only initiate interaction during play once a routine has been established? ▪ Does the child discriminate which peer(s) or adult(s) he or she allows to participate in play? ▪ How does the child react when the routine is changed? ▪ Does the child understand abstraction for jokes and humor in play?
Objects/Toys	▪ Is the child motivated and shown the ability to choose toys? ▪ What are the child's toy preferences (e.g., spinning toys; moving toys; action figures; toys of a particular size, shape, texture, or color)? ▪ Are the toy preferences consistent with the level of social engagement in the task? ▪ Do the toy preferences also reflect a clear activity preferences pattern in the child (e.g., quiet/solitary play vs. cooperative play vs. roughhouse play)? ▪ How does the child interact with toys (e.g., functionally, repetitively lining up, spinning)? ▪ Can the child play with the toy in multiple ways? ▪ Are there consistent sensory qualities to the toys a child selects (e.g., texture, vibration, lights, movement)? ▪ What motor skills are required for the toys selected in play?
Developmental/ Cognitive	▪ Does the child initiate play or only respond? ▪ Does the child make choices? ▪ Does the child have sustained attention to a play activity? ▪ How does the child's attention span vary from preferred to nonpreferred activities? ▪ Does the child have cognitive flexibility to play with objects in multiple ways and/or change or expand a play activity? ▪ How does the child handle transitions within and between activities? ▪ How does the child respond to frustration? ▪ What is the child's general level of play skill development (e.g., constructive, symbolic, role, pretend)?

and occasionally in combination with a formalized measure (see Table 5). Because a child's play performance is influenced by the surrounding environment, it is ideal to observe play across settings, both indoors and outdoors. Therapists also should observe the child in both free and structured play situations and note similarities and differences in independent play versus play with peers. These observations should describe situations in which the child interacts with, socially references, and/or imitates others. Observations also should be made regarding how much structure and consistency the child requires for interaction.

In addition to the social responding aspects of play noted above, therapists should observe the child's interactions with objects and toys in the environment. The child's ability to initiate play with a toy, explore many toys, and/or sustain play with a toy for an extended period of time also should be monitored. With these noted, assessments may be made about what motivates the child in play and what types of play interactions he or she initiates. The purposefulness or functionality of the play with objects may be evaluated in relation to the overall level of play (e.g., symbolic, creative/imaginary, pretend). For example, although the child may

Table 5. Selected Evaluation Instruments of Occupational Performance for Individuals With an ASD

Domain of Occupational Therapy	Sample Assessments Used in Occupational Therapy Practice
Areas of Occupation ■ Activities of Daily Living ■ Instrumental Activities of Daily Living ■ Rest and Sleep ■ Education ■ Work ■ Play ■ Leisure ■ Social Participation	■ Canadian Occupational Performance Measure (Law et al., 2005) ■ Perceived Efficacy and Goal Setting System (Missiuna et al., 2004) ■ Children's Assessment of Participation and Enjoyment and Preferences for Activities of Children (King et al., 2005) ■ Communication and Symbolic Behavior Scales–Developmental Profile (Wetherby & Prizant, 2002) ■ Children's Engagement Questionnaire (McWilliam, 1991) ■ Revised Knox Preschool Play Scale (Knox, 2008) ■ Play Preference Inventory (Wolfberg, 1995) ■ Test of Playfulness (Skard & Bundy, 2008) ■ Transdisciplinary Play-Based Assessment, 2nd ed. (Linder, 2008) ■ Screening Tool for Autism in Two-Year-Olds (Stone et al., 2000) ■ Autism Diagnostic Observation Schedule (Lord et al., 2002) ■ Pediatric Evaluation of Disability Inventory (Haley et al., 1992) ■ Scales of Independent Behavior–Revised (Bruininks et al., 1997) ■ Vineland Adaptive Behavior Scales–Second Edition (Sparrow et al., 2005) ■ Adaptive Behavior Assessment System, 2nd ed. (Harrison & Oakland, 2003) ■ Adaptive Behavior Assessment System–School, 2nd ed. (Harrison & Oakland, 2003) ■ WEE-FIM II (Uniform Data Systems, 2003) ■ School Function Assessment (Coster et al., 1998) ■ School Version of the Assessment of Motor and Process Skills (Fisher et al., 2005) ■ Miller Function and Participation Scales (Miller, 2006) ■ Minnesota Handwriting Test (Reisman, 1999) ■ Evaluation Tool of Children's Handwriting (Amundson, 1995) ■ Test of Handwriting Skills (Gardner, 1998)
Performance Skills ■ Sensory Perceptual Skills ■ Motor and Praxis Skills ■ Emotional Regulation Skills ■ Cognitive Skills ■ Communication and Social Skills	■ Peabody Developmental Motor Scales, 2nd ed. (Folio & Fewell, 2000) ■ Bruininks–Oseretsky Test of Motor Proficiency, 2nd ed. (Bruininks & Bruininks, 2005) ■ Motor-Free Visual Perception Test, 3rd ed. (Colarusso & Hammill, 2003) ■ Test of Visual Perceptual Skills, 3rd ed. (Martin, 2006) ■ Test of Visual Perceptual Skills–Upper Limits (Gardner, 1997) ■ Test of Visual–Motor Skills–Revised (Gardner, 1995) ■ Beery–Buktenica Developmental Test of Visual–Motor Integration (Beery et al., 2004) ■ Developmental Test of Visual Perception, 2nd ed. (Hammill et al., 1993) ■ Developmental Test of Visual Perception–Adolescent and Adult (Reynolds et al., 2002) ■ Behavior Rating Inventory of Executive Function (Gioia et al., 2000) ■ Social Responsiveness Scale (Constantino & Gruber, 2005) ■ Battelle Developmental Inventory–2nd ed. (Newborg, 2004) ■ Bayley Scales of Infant Development, 3rd ed. (Bayley, 2005) ■ Sensory Integration and Praxis Tests (Ayres, 1989) ■ Sensory Profile (Dunn, 1999) ■ Sensory Integration Inventory–Revised (Reisman & Hanschu, 1992) ■ Sensory Processing Measure: Home (Parham & Ecker, 2007); Main Classroom and School Environment Forms (Miller-Kuhaneck et al., 2007) ■ Parent Stress Index, Third Edition (Abidin, 1995)

Table 5. Selected Evaluation Instruments of Occupational Performance for Individuals With an ASD *(cont.)*

Domain of Occupational Therapy	Sample Assessments Used in Occupational Therapy Practice
Performance Patterns ■ Habits ■ Routines ■ Roles ■ Rituals	■ Canadian Occupational Performance Measure (Law et al., 2005) ■ Perceived Efficacy and Goal Setting System (Missiuna et al., 2004) ■ Children's Assessment of Participation and Enjoyment and Preferences for Activities of Children (King et al., 2005)
Contexts and Environments ■ Cultural ■ Physical ■ Social ■ Personal ■ Temporal ■ Virtual	■ Canadian Occupational Performance Measure (Law et al., 2005) ■ Perceived Efficacy and Goal Setting System (Missiuna et al., 2004) ■ Children's Assessment of Participation and Enjoyment and Preferences for Activities of Children (King et al., 2005)

feed a baby or comb its hair in a structured play routine or with prompting, his pretend play may be repetitive, without a natural evolution into more elaborate scenarios seen in typical, same-age peers. These observations also provide further insight into the child's ability for social skills such as turn taking and sharing and cognitive skills for problem solving, attention, and concentration.

The above observations not only begin to describe a child's play skill development but also provide insight into the social, motor, and sensory processing functions of a child. This information allows for a better understanding of a child's motivation to participate in testing and provides guidance for utilization of a formal measure of play (e.g., Communication and Symbolic Behavior Scales–Developmental Profile [Wetherby & Prizant, 2002]; Play Preference Inventory [Wolfberg, 1995]; Revised Knox Preschool Play Scale [Knox, 2008]; Test of Playfulness [Skard & Bundy, 2008]; Transdisciplinary Play-Based Assessment, 2nd ed. [Linder, 2008]). Additionally, these observations also guide further assessment of performance skills potentially impacting play.

School occupations. Analysis of relevant school occupations will depend on a number of factors, including the grade level of the child, school type (e.g., Montessori vs. traditional model), and the classroom placement (i.e., self-contained vs. inclusion) in the school.

Initial history gathering with the family and school personnel guides this analysis and prioritizes specific areas in which the child is experiencing difficulties. Observations of the child while participating in the activities in relevant contexts identifies the child's functional limitations, if any, and the types and level of support needed for successful participation. Observed and reported differences in participation in different settings (home vs. school) are noted.

To supplement observations, an evaluation tool also may be used. In early school-aged children, the School Function Assessment (SFA; Coster et al., 1998) can be used to measure a student's performance of functional tasks that support his or her participation in the academic and social aspects of an elementary school program (K–6). The SFA is a judgment-based assessment that is completed by one or more school professionals who know the student and his or her participation in the academic program well. The child's consistency of performance in physical and cognitive–behavioral school functions is compared to his peers in the same classroom. An alternative, the *School Version of the Assessment of Motor and Process Skills* (School AMPS; Fisher et al., 2005) can be used for children ages 3–12 years to measure a student's schoolwork task performance in typical classroom settings. The School AMPS is a naturalistic, observation-based assessment conducted in the context of a student's regular classroom during his or her typical routine while the student performs schoolwork tasks assigned by the teacher. The School AMPS enables practitioners to provide a standardized measure of a student's school motor skills and school process ability—measures of the quality of a student's schoolwork performance.

Adaptive behavior and ADLs. The child's level of performance in ADLs is another important area of assessment. Similar to the assessment of other areas of participation, both clinical observations and formal measures are used in this process, with the setting influencing the extent to which each of these methods is used. In home and community settings where the occupational therapist has sustained interaction with the family and ongoing intervention is planned, a greater emphasis may be placed on direct observation; at a diagnostic center where a child is likely to be seen for a one-time service, evaluation of ADL performance may rely more heavily on a formal measure. Most published evaluations of adaptive behavior (e.g., Adaptive Behavior Assessment System–Second Edition [Harrison & Oakland, 2003]; Pediatric Evaluation of Disability Inventory [Haley et al., 1992]; Scales of Independent Behavior–Revised [Bruininks et al., 1997]; Vineland Adaptive Behavior Scales–Second Edition [Sparrow et al., 2005]) use parental report. Supplemental interviews with the child's caregivers provide specific information about their daily living concerns and priorities.

Analysis of Performance Skills and Patterns

Current practice parameters derived from the AAN (Filipek et al., 2000), AACAP (Volkmar et al., 1999), APA (Johnson et al., 2007), and a consensus panel with representation from multiple professionals societies, including AOTA (Filipek et al., 1999), highlight the specialized role of occupational therapists in evaluating motor performance skills and sensory processing of children with an ASD. Therefore, additional discussion of these areas is warranted. For the purpose of this section, assessment of motor function will be divided into the broad areas of gross and fine/visual–motor development. A discussion of assessment of visual perception and sensory processing will follow. Each

section will discuss formal measurement of these areas and include discussion of supplemental clinical observations to be taken into account during play-based assessment and administration of standardized testing.

Integrated body functions (e.g., muscle tone, strength, coordination, visual–motor integration) serve as the foundation for skilled motor output. These body functions also have dependent relationships across motor skill areas. For example, stability aspects of gross motor development are important in fine motor performance, because stability provides a solid foundation from which skilled upper extremity usage is achieved. Similarly, sensory processing and motor skills are highly related, in that sensory feedback is essential to accurate movement.

In addition to the assessment of developmental milestones, special attention must be directed to the qualitative dimensions of motor performance. Developmental milestones provide evidence of what the child can and cannot do; however, evaluation and assessment of skills and performance patterns go beyond these aspects and attempt to determine the source of an observed and documented limitation in performance. Observations made regarding the qualitative aspects of motor control often can pinpoint the areas causing functional limitations and serve as the foundation for intervention planning. In addition to the value of direct observation of motor skills, observation of contextual aspects of motor skills also enhances understanding of the source of developmental delays. Several questions can guide this observation process:

- Does the child perform motor tasks only to seek sensory input?
- Do motor skills vary greatly depending on attention and motivation?
- Are motor skills performed only after demonstrated by the evaluator?
- Is the child's developmental pattern uneven?
- Does the child demonstrate a pattern of scattered skills in gross (e.g., climbing) or fine motor (e.g., constructional praxis, puzzle completion) domains?

It is important to gather information and observations about these areas within the context of everyday naturalistic environments. A change in environment alone or minor changes in the equipment used, such as when testing in a clinic environment, often influences motor performance in individuals with an ASD.

Gross motor skills. Gross motor assessment includes evaluation of postural stability, mobility, gross motor skills, and neurodevelopment. Neuromuscular status assessment is also a component of the child's gross motor status. Assessment of gross motor performance is often done within the context of play-based assessment or strictly through observation. Having a child go through a simple obstacle course, for instance, can provide a wealth of information regarding underlying balance, strength, motor planning, and postural control. Further, within many clinic settings or natural environments, children have the opportunity to explore the environment. In doing so, the child may demonstrate ambulation, running, jumping, and stair climbing. Supplemental reports of functioning during higher level bilateral motor tasks such as riding a bike

and swimming can be obtained from the caregiver if not seen in a natural environment with access to these skills.

Occupational therapists assess developmental milestones and observe and analyze the quality with which they are accomplished. Standardized measures of motor performance, such as the Peabody Developmental Motor Scales–Second Edition (Folio & Fewell, 2000) and the Bruininks–Oseretsky Test of Motor Proficiency, Second Edition (Bruininks & Bruininks, 2005) provide a foundation for determining the appropriateness of more specialized measures of motor performance.

Fine and visual–motor skills. During fine motor assessment, grasp of objects, writing, block play, cutting tasks, and dexterity while manipulating clothing fasteners are evaluated. Stable positioning during fine and visual–motor tasks enhances optimal performance. Many of the foundational areas relating to fine motor task performance are assessed though observation of play. Table 6 outlines some example questions to guide

Table 6. Structured Observations of Fine Motor Performance

Foundation Area	Example Observations

Hand Dominance	▪ Does the child demonstrate use of a dominant hand, mixed dominance, or ambiguous dominance?
	▪ If the child has mixed or no dominance:
	  ▪ Does he or she avoid crossing midline?
	  ▪ Does he or she consistently accomplish certain tasks (e.g., self-feeding, color) with one hand?

Grasp and Prehension Patterns	▪ Does the child have adequate hand strength to hold onto objects? ▪ Does the child have difficulty grading pressure (too much or too little) when holding objects? ▪ Can the child isolate finger motions to pick up smaller objects? ▪ Does the quality of the child's grasp and prehension abilities differ when he or she is grasping or manipulating an object vs. using the object in a functional task?
Manipulation Skill	▪ What is the quality of the child's in-hand manipulation skill? ▪ Can the child transition objects in his or her hand utilizing transverse palmar (palm-to-finger and finger-to-palm) motions, or does he or she stabilize the object against the table or him- or herself and regrasp? ▪ Does the child demonstrate different manipulation abilities when he or she is grasping, carrying, or manipulating an object vs. using the object in a functional task?
Purposes and Quality of a Child's Interactions With Objects	▪ Does the child manipulate objects primarily for sensory gratification or for purposeful toy play? ▪ Are tremors present, or do the child's movements appear ataxic? ▪ Does the child have a hard time damping his or her reach? ▪ Does the child frequently shift his or her position while interacting with an object, or does he or she frequently turn or reposition a task? ▪ If so, is he or she doing so to avoid midline crossing or for visual inspection? ▪ Does the child use peripheral vision or central vision, or does he or she accomplish tasks "by feel"?

these structured observations during fine motor assessment. Administration of standardized measures and observations of supplemental engagement in purposeful tasks are used to identify strengths, weaknesses, and developmental levels. If the child is unable to perform a fine motor task, activity analysis will allow the practitioner to determine related factors, including weakness, deficient muscle control, dyspraxia, cognitive limitations, or lack of motivation.

Fine motor performance and visual–motor control are linked to intact visual localization, visual tracking, and somatosensory abilities and are fundamental to many school occupations (e.g., writing, drawing, cutting on a line, catching a ball, coloring, printing). Perceptual–motor tasks that rely on spatial awareness (e.g., puzzles, formboards) are often a strength for children with an ASD; less structured tasks that involve motor planning (e.g., drawing, handwriting, cutting) are often more difficult. Some individuals may demonstrate better abilities for design by copying items in tests of visual–motor integration (e.g., Developmental Test of Visual–Motor Integration, 5th Edition [Beery et al., 2004], Test of Visual–Motor Skills–Revised [Gardner, 1995]) but have difficulty during language-based activities when relating these abilities when evaluating handwriting (e.g., Evaluation Tool of Children's Handwriting [Amundson, 1995], Minnesota Handwriting Assessment [Reisman, 1999], Test of Handwriting Skills [Gardner, 1998]). Therefore, it is important to assess each skill area separately.

Fundamental to assessment is the recurrent theme of pinpointing where the breakdown in task performance has taken place. In the visual–motor area, skills are dependent on adequate attention, visual perception, motor control, and motivation. Questions to ask when analyzing performance deficits include

- Is the child visually attending to the activity?
- Are any noted visual–perceptual deficits affecting performance?
- Does the problem appear to relate more to visual processing or motor control?
- Is this a novel task?
- Is performance better in structured vs. unstructured tasks?
- Does the child lack interest in the task?

Visual perception. In conjunction with fine and visual–motor assessment, visual discrimination, visual memory, visual form constancy, visual–spatial relation, visual–sequential memory, visual figure ground, and visual–closure perceptual areas often are evaluated. Together, these perceptual skills allow us to use visual information to recognize, recall, discriminate, and make meaning out of what we see and provide vital information that is utilized and relied on by many other systems for optimal functioning.

Formalized assessment of visual–perceptual abilities in autism is usually reserved for children of school age and older who have adequate receptive-language abilities to allow the child to comprehend the required verbal instructions. Visual–perceptual instruments (see Table 5) assess nonmotor perception, in that they do not require motor coordination for the completion of testing. Instead, the child can select his or her choice among the options by saying or pointing to the appropriate letter, form, or design that corresponds to his selection.

Supplemental clinical observations can be used to obtain informal information about perceptual abilities in children who cannot participate in formal testing. Practitioners can devise situations to assess specific areas or evaluate a child's work. For instance, having a child find a particular toy in a toy box can functionally assess visual figure ground, and asking a child to find or select an item he was shown can be used to assess visual memory. Spatial relations difficulties may be seen when a child asked to write on lined paper rotates drawings, letters, or words.

Sensory processing. Another specialized area of evaluation for an occupational therapist is sensory processing. Similar to many other aspects of the evaluation process with an individual with an ASD, both formal and informal measures are used. Standardized caregiver or teacher reports include the Sensory Profile (Dunn, 1999), Sensory Integration Inventory–Revised (Reisman & Hanschu, 1992), and Sensory Processing Measure, Home Form (Parham & Ecker, 2007) and Main Classroom and School Environment (Miller-Kuhaneck et al., 2007) forms. These inventories gather information regarding sensory processing within daily life situations, measuring the child's responsivity to varied sensory experiences (e.g., tactile, auditory, visual, vestibular, gustatory) and include assessment of behavior, praxis, and emotional lability. The scores can be graphed to depict the child's pattern of responses. In addition to a caregiver report measure, the Sensory Integration and Praxis Tests (Ayres, 1989) may be administered by a certified therapist to gather more specialized information. However, use of this instrument is rare and requires that the child has good receptive language.

Assessment of sensory processing includes structured clinical observations and response to sensory experiences. Because the environment and/or the contents of that environment can change how an indi-

vidual responds to sensory input, these observations may support the caregiver report or provide contrasting information about the effects of an individual's sensory processing within different environments. It is important to note the sensory qualities of that environment (e.g., size and openness of the space, light quality and type, heating/ventilation noise, room temperature, visual qualities, smells) during the evaluation. These environmental conditions alone may impact an individual's ability to successfully participate in his or her daily occupations. Additional structured observations during evaluation of sensory processing and praxis in individuals with an ASD are found in Table 7 and may be guided more formally with use of *Observations Based on Sensory Integration Theory* (Blanche, 2002).

Table 7. Structured Observations During Evaluation of Sensory Processing

Observation Area	Pertinent Questions
Patterns of Self-Regulation Within Each Environment	• What does the individual do to calm, arouse, and/or organize his or her behavior? • What tasks or environments have a natural calming or arousing effect on the child? • Does the child appear to seek sensory input through movement, self-vocalizing, mouthing of objects, rocking, or hand flapping? • Does the child show a preference for either open or tight places? • Are there tactile, auditory, visual, and vestibular events or parts of activities that the child avoids?
Attention to Task Performance	• Does the child demonstrate sustained attention to certain tasks or tasks with a specific sensory component (e.g., visually stimulating or tactile tasks)? • How does incorporating sensory input into nonpreferred tasks alter the child's attention and engagement?
Changes in Social Behavior	• Does the child demonstrate differing degrees of joint attention, eye contact, shared enjoyment, and/or social referencing with changes in sensory events? • Does the child show a pattern of proximity (e.g., leaning, touching, movement away) in relation to others (peers or adults) that could relate to sensory processing?
Impact of the Environment on Praxis	• Does a change in equipment/media impair the child's ability to or quality with which he completes a task? • What support or assistance (e.g., touch cues, visual supports, task demonstration) in the environment assists the child most? • Does the child spontaneously imitate social behavior or motor movement? • Can the child imitate a demonstrated motor movement and is his or her ability to imitate dependent on the presence of a verbal component? • Is there an environment in which the child consistently demonstrates optimal participation in occupations?
Quality of Movement Differences Between Familiar and Novel Tasks	• Are spontaneous/reflexive movements more fluid than movements on verbal command? • Does the child have difficulty with task initiation, sequencing, or both?

Together, these formal and structured observation measures of sensory processing provide the basis for program and intervention planning. These sensory processing deficits are often the primary focus of treatment reported by occupational therapists working with individuals with ASDs (Case-Smith & Miller, 1999).

Contexts and Environments

Occupational therapists acknowledge the influence of cultural, physical, social, personal, temporal, and virtual contextual factors on occupations and activities. Therefore, factors that support or inhibit performance should be identified during the evaluation process. Because the symptoms of autism are highly influenced by the environment, analysis of behavior in the natural environment is desirable. Observation in multiple settings can provide significant information about how a child functions and how the differences in settings change behavior and performance (Ozonoff et al., 2005). Thus, the context in which evaluation of occupational performance occurs is an essential consideration. Table 3 summarizes activity demands and contextual considerations for assessment.

Activity Demands

Determining whether a child may be able to complete an activity depends not only on the performance skills, performance patterns, and client factors but also on the demands of the activity itself. The demands of an activity are aspects of the activity that include the tools needed to carry out an activity; the space and social demands required by the activity; and the skills, body functions, and body structures needed to take part in a given activity (AOTA, 2008b).

Client Factors

The activity demands of childhood occupations require a child to have adequate cognitive, sensory, and motor control. Assessment of these client factors (e.g., body functions) can inform the occupational therapist about the client's ability to engage in occupations.

Interpretation of Evaluation Results

As can be seen in the previous discussion, the evaluation of individuals with ASDs and their families is multifaceted. As such, the identified strengths and weaknesses of the individual also likely will be diverse. The evaluation process is not fully complete, however, until the therapist interprets the evaluation findings. Ultimately, if deficits are noted in any of the underlying factors and aspects within the domain of occupational therapy, yet they do not impair occupational performance, services may not be warranted. After collecting the evaluation data, the practitioner integrates evaluation information to obtain a clear understanding of the individual performance and participation. After the occupational therapist interprets the evaluation data, these evaluation findings are integrated with the evaluation results of other team members. This integration provides a comprehensive description of the individual's strengths, identifies the underlying impairments that limit participation, and leads to an intervention plan. When conducting evidence-based practice, a third level of integration guides intervention planning. Much of the rest of this guideline focuses directly on the development and implementation of evidence-based intervention programs for individuals with an ASD.

Intervention

Occupational therapy practitioners use the information about the child and his or her family gathered during the evaluation to direct client-centered and occupation-based interventions. The intervention process consists of the skilled actions taken by occupational therapy practitioners in collaboration with the child and other care providers to facilitate engagement in occupation related to health and participation (AOTA, 2008b). This intervention process is divided into three steps: (1) plan, (2) implementation, and (3) review. During the intervention process, information from the evaluation is integrated with theory, practice, frames of reference, intervention methods, and evidence from the literature. This information guides the clinical reasoning of the occupational therapist in the development, implementation, and review of the intervention plan.

Intervention Plan and Implementation

The occupational therapy practitioner develops the intervention plan collaboratively with the client; the plan is based on the client's goals and priorities. Depending on whether the client is a person, organization, or population, others, such as family members, significant others, board members, service providers, and community groups, also may collaborate in the development of the plan. The selection and design of the intervention plan and goals are directed toward addressing the client's current and potential problems related to engagement in occupations and/or activities.

The design of the intervention plan is directed by the (1) client's goals, values, and beliefs; (2) client's health and well-being; (3) client's performance skills and performance patterns; (4) collective influence of activity demands, client factors, and the context, which includes the environment, on the client; (5) context of service delivery in which the intervention is provided; and (6) best available evidence. Several of these considerations specifically will be highlighted in this discussion of intervention planning.

In addition to the above considerations, intervention planning for children on the autism spectrum often is complicated by the need to integrate occupational therapy interventions into the context of other interventions the child may be receiving. Typically, children with an ASD receive multiple, concurrent interventions within various settings (Aman, 2005; Levy & Hyman, 2003). For instance, curriculum goals for a child within the academic environment may be facilitated through the use of principles of discrete trial training and structured teaching, while the child also participates in ongoing speech–language intervention to facilitate communication skill development, peer-modeling for social skill training, and occupational therapy intervention targeting participation. Outside the academic environment, the same child may receive additional behavioral (e.g., applied behavioral analysis) and biomedical interventions (e.g., gluten- and casein-

free diet, vitamin supplements). Collaborative efforts can begin when professionals become aware of and gain an understanding of the myriad interventions in which children with autism may participate. Primary interventions implemented by occupational therapy practitioners are described on pages 31–44.

Intervention Review and Outcome Monitoring

Intervention review is a continuous process of reevaluating and reviewing the intervention plan, the effectiveness of its delivery, and the progress toward targeted outcomes (AOTA, 2008b). This regular monitoring of the results of occupational therapy intervention determines the need to continue or modify the intervention plan, discontinue intervention, provide follow-up, or refer the client to other agencies or professionals. Reevaluation may involve readministering assessments used at the time of initial evaluation, a satisfaction questionnaire completed by the client, or questions that evaluate each goal. Reevaluation normally substantiates progress toward goal attainment, indicates any change in functional status, and directs modification to the intervention plan, if necessary (Moyers & Dale, 2007). Additionally, this review of intervention may require revisiting available literature if occupational performance of the individual has changed.

Intervention review for individuals with an ASD is an ongoing process, with the setting and context again playing a significant role. For example, practitioners working in natural environments in early intervention programs conduct ongoing assessment as part of the intervention process. Here, family outcomes written on the individualized family service plan are monitored. In addition to these child-specific outcomes, the occupational therapist also contributes developmental reassessment components to the state-level child outcome reporting system for indicators within the State Performance Plan and Annual Performance Report required by the U.S. Office of Special Education Programs (U.S. OSEP, 2006).

Intervention review and outcome monitoring in the public schools for children receiving occupational therapy services under IDEA are completed formally

marized in Appendix C. The research studies presented here include Level I randomized controlled trials; Level II studies, in which assignment to a treatment or a control group is not randomized (cohort study); and Level III studies, which do not have a control group. For the purposes of this review, only Level I, II, and III studies are included. Themes of relevance to occupational therapy that were consistent across the studies are presented and represent the foundation components in the development of all intervention programs.

Sensory integration and sensory-based interventions.

Most children with autism exhibit behaviors that indicate sensory modulation disorders. *Sensory modulation* refers to the central nervous system's ability to regulate its own activity (Ayres, 1979) and is a complex process by which neural messages about the intensity, frequency, duration, complexity, and novelty of sensory stimulation are perceived (Miller & Lane, 2000). Certain children with autism appear to be overly responsive (*hyperresponsive*) to typical sensory input, while others appear to be underresponsive (*hyposensitive*).

Behaviors associated with sensory modulation disorders include overly active, negative, impulsive, or aggressive responses to sensory input or withdrawal and avoidance of sensation (Miller, Anzalone, Lane, Cermak, & Osten, 2007). Sensory processing difficulties also may relate to certain self-stimulation behaviors and may be the basis for a child's difficulty in transitioning to new situations. Greenspan and Wieder (1997) documented that about 97% of the children with an ASD treated in their clinic had sensory processing problems. Similar findings were reported in a sample studied by Tomchek and Dunn (2007), in which 95% of the children with an ASD demonstrated sensory processing impairments. Others (e.g., Baranek, 2002) have documented that sensory modulation problems can interfere with the children's daily life routines and with the families' functioning. Researchers are not in agreement as to what type of sensory modulation problems are most associated with ASDs; some authors describe children as hyposensitive (particularly to auditory and vestibular input) and others as hypersensitive (particularly to tactile; Dawson & Watling, 2000; Edelson, Edelson, Kerr, & Grandin, 1999; Greenspan & Wieder, 1997). It appears that many children have both hypersensitivity and hyposensitivity and that their ability to process sensory input fluctuates. Both sensory integration and sensory-based approaches are used to improve these conditions and are described in the following sections.

Sensory integration intervention. Sensory integration has been well described in the occupational therapy literature (e.g., Ayres, 1979; Bundy, Lane, & Murray, 2002). The goal of sensory integration intervention is to improve the efficiency of the nervous system in interpreting sensory information for functional use (Parham & Mailloux, 2005). The therapist provides an environment rich in sensory experiences and offers activities that challenge the child to gradually engage in more challenging tasks and produce more complex responses. The activities developed by the therapist are developmentally appropriate, offer a "just-right" challenge to the child, and are designed to evoke an adaptive response. The adaptive response helps the child organize the sensory input and produce a functionally appropriate response to that input. The therapist supports the child's adaptive responses by monitoring the child's functional behavior; giving verbal cueing or physical support during the activity; or modifying the activity if the child becomes frustrated, overstimulated, or unsuccessful.

Parham et al. (2007) identified the components of sensory integration intervention. Following an extended fidelity study, these researchers defined sensory integration as a playful, dynamic interaction between the therapist and child that includes enhanced sensation, collaboration between child and therapist, assurance of safety by the therapist, the child's choice of activity, and the therapist's support of the child's success in the activity. The goal of the therapeutic activities is to promote the child's optimal arousal, playful interactions with adults and peers, immersion into the therapeutic play activities, and successful adaptive responses.

Children with autism also receive sensory-based interventions that emphasize the sensory input and its effect on behavior. *Vestibular stimulation* (e.g., rocking or bouncing) is often the primary sensory stimulation provided. Rotary vestibular stimulation appears to be calming for certain children and arousing for others. When used in a therapeutic context, vestibular stimulation can improve attention, increase eye contact, and help to calm and organize behavior (Mailloux, 2001). Children with autism also seem to benefit from deep touch and joint compression (Mailloux & Roley, 2004). Grandin explained how throughout her life, deep pressure has helped her to feel calm and organized (Edelson, Edelson, et al., 1999). She developed the concept of the hug machine based on her experiences as a young child seeking deep pressure. Some children seek vibration and use vibration to help them to calm or increase their arousal. Sensory-based interventions, such as enhanced vestibular and proprioceptive sensation, serve to prepare the child to focus on learning activities and to demonstrate socially appropriate behaviors.

Most sensory integration programs include two aspects: (1) clinic-based sessions, in which the child receives sensory-rich input through playful, goal-directed activities, and (2) sensory diets, daily programs implemented into the child's routines at home and school. Sensory integration intervention sessions often focus on developing specific skills and improving the child's ability to produce adaptive responses to sensory input. This intervention program is goal directed, with the therapist supporting the child's choice of activity, creating challenges, and increasing the complexity of the activities within the child's range of developmental skill.

The sensory diet is individually designed for the child by the therapist but may be monitored and reinforced by parents and teachers. The sensory diet is designed to help the child use sensory input to modulate his or her arousal levels and behavioral responses to sensation throughout the day. This program enables the child to participate in activities throughout the day by helping him or her maintain optimal arousal and avoid disorganized behaviors from overstimulation. Sensory diets most often involve specific alerting or calming activities or a retreat from sensory stimulation at regular intervals throughout the day. In a sensory

diet, sensory elements (e.g., music, neoprene vest, weighted blanket) can be added to the child's routine. Equipment and environments that promote calming or alerting responses (e.g., sitting in a beanbag chair, rocking in a rocker, hiding in a tent, sitting in a ball pit, jumping on a mini trampoline, headphones with music, brushing) are made available to the child throughout the day. In general, the goal is to help optimize the child's attention and focus and promote organized, appropriate behavior. These programs must be assessed continually to monitor effects on behaviors and make revisions based on the child's responses.

Certain sensory-based techniques are initially passive and must be provided by the therapist, parent, or teacher. These techniques may include intensive sensory stimulation to one sensory system. The Wilbarger Deep Pressure and Proprioceptive Technique (Wilbarger & Wilbarger, 1991), with a surgical brush using a stroking motion on the arms and legs, followed by the trunk, has been used with children in the autism spectrum. The brushing is combined with joint compression and must be repeated throughout the day on a regular (every 2 hours) schedule. Massage is another touch-based approach that has been used with children with autism (Field et al., 1997). This approach uses deep pressure and circular motions, and its recommended use is less frequent than brushing. For example, a clinical trial achieved effects with massage for 15 minutes, twice a week. As the child matures and improves, he or she is encouraged to independently access ways to maintain optimal arousal in socially appropriate ways (e.g., running in the morning, hot showers, weighted blankets, listening through headphones). Sensory-intensive interventions should be monitored vigilantly for immediate and long-term effects, adjusting intensity and duration of the sensory input as needed.

In occupational therapy, sensory integration or sensory-based interventions are paired with play-based or functional activities. Often, the sensory intervention is viewed as preparation for the child to participate in an activity designed to enhance specific skills (e.g., social interaction, pretend play, visual–motor performance). These skill-building activities are woven into the treat-

that includes the family, teaching, and therapy staff is needed. Occupational therapists frequently take leadership roles in these intervention approaches because the child-centered focus aligns with the approaches typically used by occupational therapists.

The goal of relationship-based interventions is to establish a positive parent–child relationship that will facilitate the child's social–emotional growth and promote development of pivotal behaviors essential for learning (e.g., joint attention, positive affect; Koegel, Koegel, & Carter, 1999). These interventions are based on the belief that behaviors exhibited by children with autism reflect unique biologically based processing difficulties that affect social interaction competence, play, and communication (Greenspan & Wieder, 2006). In developmental, relationship-based intervention, therapists model interactions that create problem-solving scenarios, encourage the child's sustained play, and support his or her responses. Parents are encouraged to increase their attentiveness to their child, improve their sensitivity to the child's communication attempts, and increase their positive responsiveness (Mahoney & Perales, 2005).

Coaching parents in how to sustain playful turn-taking has been described in the occupational therapy literature for many years (Hanft, Rush, & Sheldon, 2003). The therapist makes suggestions as to how the parent can read the child's cues, create a play activity of interest to the child, embed a dilemma in the child's play that facilitates interaction, and support that child's responses with imitation or reinforcement. Attention to and responsiveness to the child are critical aspects of this intervention method. Elements that are emphasized are selecting a play activity that is developmentally appropriate, embedding a challenge in the activity that will interest the child, and encouraging interaction. Parents are encouraged to use descriptive terms rather than directive statements, wait for the child's response, use exaggerated gestures to promote imitation, and maintain positive affect (Koegel et al., 1999; MacDonald, 1989; Mahoney & Perales, 2005). Therapists encourage the parents' interest in the activity and ability to sustain the activity (keeping the interaction going for as many turns as possible).

Research evidence on relationship-based interventions. Research has shown that interventions emphasizing responsive, supportive relationships and social–emotional development in young children can facilitate the child's social–emotional growth and promote development of pivotal behaviors (Greenspan & Wieder, 1997; Mahoney & Perales, 2005; Wieder & Greenspan, 2005). Greenspan and Wieder (1997) completed a chart review of 200 children who had participated in developmental, relationship-based floortime therapy with their parents in addition to interdisciplinary comprehensive interventions. In this one, pre- and posttest study group, client outcomes were categorized as good to outstanding (58%), medium (25%), and limited (17%). The study was primarily descriptive, identifying the types and levels of change that can be anticipated from the developmental, interaction-based approach that the authors developed. Although the study lacked controls and manipulation of participants, it provided a detailed review of cases that described the developmental course of children with ASDs. Wieder and Greenspan (2005) completed a follow-up of 16 of the children whose initial outcomes had been good to outstanding with their model of a developmental, individualized, relationship-based (DIR) intervention. The children were evaluated 10 to 15 years after the intervention. This detailed report documented that the children had become socially competent, responsive, and interactive. The symptoms that remained suggested some mental illness (depression and anxiety), but the primary characteristics of autism were no longer evident. Although their report is encouraging, it must be viewed as inconclusive evidence, in that the case descriptions suggest but do not prove the types of long-term outcomes that can be expected when early outcomes of relationship-based therapy are positive.

Mahoney and Perales (2005) completed a one-group study measuring the effects of relationship-focused intervention on young children with pervasive developmental disorders that encouraged parents (mothers) to increase their responsiveness to their children. As in the Greenspan and Wieder (1997) studies, a primary focus of the intervention was guiding parents to develop interactional skills, responsiveness, and sensitivity to their child. Following a year of the relationship-focused intervention, mothers made significant increases in responsiveness and children made significant gains in social–emotional functioning (Mahoney & Perales, 2005). These studies suggest that occupational therapists should embrace parents in their intervention, coaching them in methods that promote their child's social–emotional growth. These studies suggest that relationship-focused interventions are effective when working with young (preschool-age) children, children who seem relatively high on the spectrum, and parents who have the resources and energy to become highly involved in the intervention activities.

School-based programs. Occupational therapists often participate in comprehensive school-based programs. Their roles in these programs are supportive of the strategies designed by the team. At the same time, occupational therapists bring unique skills and perspectives to the program. Often the contributions of the occupational therapy practitioners relate to their in-depth understanding of the child's performance in the context of his or her developmental levels, unique strengths and concerns, the environment, and the activity (curriculum) demands.

In general, early childhood/preschool programs for children with autism are developmental and play based. Early childhood programs may use behavioral interventions with targeted children but not as a primary strategy for all children's learning. When students reach elementary-school age, programs emphasize functional and academic goals. In elementary school and beyond, developmental approaches are deemphasized and behavioral approaches tend to become the dominant teaching method.

Developmental, skill-based programs. Early childhood programs for young children with autism often use play-based activities to enhance children's developmental skills. These activities are specifically designed to enhance socialization, communication, play skills, and peer interaction. Developmental programs are based

on an in-depth understanding of the developmental process and the interrelationships among developmental domains. They are founded on the appreciation that biologically based individual differences must be considered in developing activities to engage the child. Intervention strategies focus on the child's foundational learning skills (e.g., sustained attention, turn-taking, initiative, persistence) that enable learning across performance areas (e.g., language, cognitive, fine motor performance). Developmental, skill-based approaches are similar to the relationship-based interventions in that they consider the child's affect, sensory modulation, motor planning, and interaction styles. When compared to relationship-based intervention, these approaches often are more comprehensive, include direct instruction, and incorporate peers into learning activities. The developmental, skill-based framework is highly consistent with occupational therapy frames of reference, and occupational therapists frequently contribute to these programs.

In developmental skill-based programs, the occupational therapy practitioner follows the child's lead, showing sustained interest in his or her activities, often imitating the child's actions (Audet, Mann, & Miller-Kuhaneck, 2004). The practitioner, on the play activity, demonstrates the next step, a higher level action, or a new challenge. The practitioner leads the child to a "just-right challenge," combining fine motor and pretend play goals. The practitioner describes the activity during interaction with the child, commenting on the pretend play scenario and occasionally making a corrective or instructive comment. The occupational therapy practitioner may present a dilemma for the child to solve. For example, the therapist might say, "The doll is tired and cold; what should we do for her?" or put a small doll's hat on the doll's foot and ask, "Is this where the hat belongs?" A combination of challenging the child to take the next step and trying a new action and encouraging practice of emerging skills is used. The goal of the occupational therapy practitioner–child interaction is beyond teaching a skill; it also motivates the child to initiate action, develop self-efficacy, engage with others, and generalize new skills to a variety of play contexts.

Rogers and DiLalla (1991) described the constructs of their developmental model. These elements are highly consistent with occupational therapy practice.

1. *Positive affect.* Positive affect, often referred to as *playfulness* in occupational therapy, is critical to learning and the development of relationships.

2. *Self-directed activity.* The child's self-directed activities in the natural environment are the basis for learning. Occupational therapy often is provided in the natural environment using a child-centered approach. For children with autism who are passive and reluctant to act, the occupational therapist can use a more directive approach (e.g., modeling and instructing) to engage the child.

3. *Social interaction.* Play-based programs focus on social interaction as the critical goal. The occupational therapy practitioner uses small group activities with typical peers to promote social interaction. Methods to enhance interaction include activities that allow peer modeling, turn-taking, and sharing. Use of playful turn-taking activities promotes the child's engagement.

4. *Consistent structure.* A consistent daily structure is used. The occupational therapy practitioner follows this structure and consistently communicates to the child what activity comes next. The practitioner helps the child work through changes in the routine.

This approach requires that activities are developmentally appropriate and individualized. The involvement of peers as models and tutors is also an important element. Because children with autism exhibit inappropriate behaviors at times, the team adopts consistent ways to handle disruptive behaviors. Usually these approaches are positive and involve brief removal from the group and instructing alternative, more desirable behaviors (Rogers & DiLalla, 1991).

Research evidence on developmental skill-based programs. The Denver Model is a primary example of the developmental, play-based program. In a one-group study using pre- and posttest comparisons, Rogers, Herbison, Lewis, Pantone, and Reis (1986) collected assessment data on 26 children who attended the Denver Model program for at least 6 months. The program ran 4 half-days a week in classes of 6 children with 1 teacher and 2 aides. Psychotherapists and speech–language pathologists provided consultation but not direct services. The children were compared at the beginning and end of the 6 months on developmental skills, symbolic play, and social–communicative play skills. In addition, parent–child interactions were evaluated. The children improved significantly in cognitive, language, and social–emotional performance. They also improved in play skills. Parent–child interaction did not change. At a follow-up evaluation, one-third of the children entered regular education, and two-thirds continued to receive special education services.

Rogers and DiLalla (1991) compared the effects of the Denver Model on children with autism and on children with other developmental disorders. After 6 to 9 months of intervention, the children with autism made significant progress in all areas of developmental delay measured and made similar progress to that of the comparison group of children with developmental disorders.

Kasari, Freeman, and Paparella (2006) used an approach similar to the Denver Model, although they added a brief initial behavioral component. Children (mean age 42 months) were randomly assigned to a group that emphasized joint attention ($n = 20$), one that emphasized play ($n = 21$), or a control group ($n = 17$). The researchers used discrete trial training for 5 to 8 minutes, then implemented a natural, play-based approach for the remainder of the session (22–25 additional minutes). In the play-based approach, the researchers followed the child's lead, imitated the child, and adapted the activity to allow the child's success. These procedures were implemented daily within an early intervention program for 5 to 6 weeks.

The dependent variables were joint attention, imitation skills, and symbolic play. All of the children whose intervention focused on joint attention improved in joint attention that generalized to other environments. The children gave toys, showed toys, and coordinated joint looks more than the comparison group. The group with play goals exhibited higher levels of symbolic play and mastery level of play. This

Box 1. Implications of Developmental, Play-Based Interventions for Occupational Therapy

These developmental, play-based interventions are consistent with occupational therapy approaches. An advantage appears to be that they are easily applied to the child's natural environments, such as a day care center or early childhood program. Because they are implemented in the natural environment (e.g., the early childhood education program), they are consistent with the legal mandate for education in the least restrictive environment (Individuals With Disabilities Education Act, 2004). Occupational therapists who participate in these interventions need to use a collaborative, in-class, integrated model of services. In-class service delivery models allow therapists to access peers, use the child's familiar play activities, and collaborate with the teaching staff in activity choice and curricular goal.

study demonstrated the effectiveness of a combined behavioral and developmental program to improve joint attention and symbolic play. See Box 1 for implications for occupational therapists. Kasari and colleagues (2006) also demonstrated that intervention effects in the classroom could generalize to interactions with parents at home.

Elementary school programs: TEACCH. As students enter elementary school, the curricular focus switches from social and physical play skills to an emphasis on academic and functional performance. One comprehensive approach used in school is Treatment and Education of Autistic and Communication Handicapped Children (TEACCH). Developed in the 1970s by Eric Schopler, (Schopler, Mesibov, Shigley, & Bashford, 1984) TEACCH is a structured learning approach that involves organizing the environment and presenting clear, concrete visual information to guide students' behaviors and actions. The program reflects an eclectic approach that uses both developmental and behavioral theories. The learning materials are selected and activities developed on the basis of individual assessment of the child's strengths, limitations, learning style, and interests and of an understanding of how autism affects behavior and learning. Visual strategies are emphasized because these tend to be strengths for individuals with autism. Teachers develop the activities based on the student's interests; for example, they may use the child's interest in letters, puzzles, or trains to teach math or language concepts.

The program is generally implemented in a full-day instructional program in which the environment is structured into well-organized tasks. Visual schedules for the day help the child transition from one activity to another, and visual cues guide the child through his or her learning activities. Routines are established and consistently maintained. Rather than providing an immediate positive reward to the child's response, completion of the task is in and of itself motivating. This aspect of TEACCH may lead to optimal generalization and is consistent with occupational therapy interventions.

Research evidence on TEACCH effectiveness. TEACCH programs most often are implemented in schools (see Box 2); however, the strategies can be implemented in a home program. Ozonoff and Cathcart (1998) analyzed the effects of a TEACCH-based home program. Two nonrandomized groups of children with autism were compared. Eleven children, ages 2–6, were in each group. The home program was 10 weeks in length and was implemented by parents. The focus was use of visual strategies and developmentally appropriate activities. The group in the TEACCH intervention improved more in imitation, fine motor, gross motor, and cognitive performance on the Psycho-Educational Profile–Revised (PEP–R; Schopler, Reichler, Bashford, Lansing, & Marcus, 1990). Limitations of the study were lack of randomization and lack of a follow-up measure.

In a more recent study in Italy, Panerai, Ferrante, and Zingale (2002) compared a TEACCH program with a control group in a traditional program. Two groups of 8 children with autism (mean age 9 years) were compared. The TEACCH program focused on adapting the child's environment and establishing methods for alternative communication. The pro-

Box 2. Implications of the TEACCH Program for Occupational Therapy

Encouraging students to actively participate in classroom routines can prevent nonpurposeful or disruptive behaviors. When occupational therapists use visual schedules in their treatments, they have a method to transition the student from activity to activity, keeping the student focused. The student can see what activity comes next, which can motivate him or her to complete the current activity. Occupational therapy practitioners use visual schedules, picture exchange communication systems, computer games, and visual cueing to promote students' participation in the classroom. To generalize students' learning in the classroom to their home environment, occupational therapists can assist parents in developing visual schedules and establishing structured daily routines at home (Watling, 2004).

grams were implemented for 1 year, and the PEP–R was administered at the beginning and end of the intervention. The TEACCH group made significant gains when pre- and posttest measures were compared. When groups were compared, eye–hand coordination was the only skill area significantly higher in the TEACCH group. On the Vineland Adaptive Behavior Scales (Sparrow et al., 1984), the TEACCH group improved more than the control in personal daily living, play and leisure, and total scores. Although the TEACCH group performed better, these differences were modest. The participants had significant cognitive delays that may have accounted for their overall modest rate of improvement.

Social skills interventions. Structured social interaction groups. As described in the first section of this guideline, a defining characteristic of children with autism is minimal initiation of and difficulty sustaining social interaction. Reasons for their delays in learning social skills include limited understanding of nonverbal cues, limited ability to read facial expressions, and difficulty interpreting communication. Their limited social skills do not necessarily reflect lack of interest in their peers. Occupational therapists assess a child's social skills to determine the individual factors that relate to social skill delays, including poor eye contact, difficulty in auditory processing, sensory processing disorders, and limited understanding of social cues and gestures. Assessment of sensory, cognitive, perceptual, and language performance as these factors relate to social function forms the basis for the child's individualized program.

One strategy used by occupational therapy practitioners to enhance social participation in students with autism is to create and run groups that meet during the school day and focus on social skills. Greene (2004) described activity-based social skills groups for children with autism. These groups have established rules and consistent formats. The occupational therapist selects activities that create a milieu for interaction and enable children to learn and practice social skills. For example, the occupational therapist may design a cooking activity for a small group of students in which each student has a particular job and the group has to work together to successfully complete the task. The practitioner may design a craft activity or construction project in which the students need to share materials and each contribute to the final outcome. During the activity, the practitioner models, encourages, and reinforces turn-taking, sharing materials, communication with emphasis on pragmatics, social rules, and expression of feelings. When possible, the group includes students without autism so that peer modeling and initiation of interaction support the social behaviors of the students with autism. The group should relate to the social challenges that the students face in the classroom so that the behaviors easily generalize to the classroom (Greene, 2004).

Research evidence on social interaction groups. Several studies examined the effects of social games and interactive activities with peers on children's development of social behaviors and communication skills (LeGoff, 2004; LeGoff & Sherman, 2006; Schleien, Mustonen, & Rynders, 1995). Two quasi-experimental studies examined the effects of Lego® therapy on social competence in elementary-aged children with autism (LeGoff, 2004; LeGoff & Sherman, 2006). The intervention was similar to occupational therapy activity groups in that simple social rules for playing were established, the focus was on cooperative play and fun, peers and aides facilitated the play with cueing and modeling, members participated in joint decisions, and families were given information and resources. Lego blocks were selected because children with autism often have an affinity for constructing with blocks and prefer structured activities. The leaders gave the groups a specific design to build, which automatically structured the activity and required that the children interact and cooperate. The intervention was developed through pilot work that included feedback from the students and parents. The elements of the intervention included: (1) social rules, (2) rewards for appropriate social behaviors, (3) participation of siblings as helpers, (4) use of therapeutic aides, (5) structured sessions that included free playtime, (6) joint decision making, and (7) a support network for the families. Following 12 weeks of twice-a-week intervention, the measures showed that the intervention group, compared to a control condition, was significantly higher in social initiation and duration of social interactions (LeGoff, 2004).

In a follow-up study (Legoff & Sherman, 2006), a matched sample of children was compared to a group who had participated in Lego therapy for a 3-year period. The Lego therapy group improved more in social interaction than the control group. Children who initially were higher in language made greater gains during the intervention. These studies demonstrate that social activity–based groups that provide a consistent structure for interaction can improve the social competence of children with autism. Elements that seem to be important to the groups include social rules for cooperation, selection of materials of interest to the children, facilitation of sharing and turn-taking, and support of families and peers. Modeling of social behaviors and reinforcement of appropriate social responses also appear to be important elements of this intervention.

Hwang and Hughes (2000) completed a comparative review to examine the effects of naturalistic social interactive interventions on increasing children's social–communicative skills, particularly their initiation of social interactions. The focus of this review was research on naturalistic interventions such as contingent imitation, naturally occurring reinforcement, and arranging the environment to increase the child's interest in activities. The authors seemed interested in both relationship-based and social–interactive interventions, recognizing that these approaches have a similar conceptual basis. Hwang and Hughes reviewed 16 studies that included 64 children (average age 6.5 years). Most of the studies used single-subject designs (primarily multiple baseline or reversal design) with the child serving as his or her own control.

The outcomes examined were social behavior, such as requesting assistance, greetings, eye gaze, joint attention, and imitation. The analysis reported results for specific strategies, many of which can be used by occupational therapists. By waiting for a child to respond (long pause before cueing again), children exhibited increases in verbal responses. Arranging the environment to present challenges to the child (e.g., placing favorite toy on high shelf) increased communication attempts. Imitating the children drew in their eye gaze and resulted in positive affect and attending. Several studies in the review reported generalization of skills and maintenance of positive findings. This review was unique in that it identified specific strategies across studies that seemed to be effective. These simple strategies (e.g., waiting for the child to respond, placing the child in a situation in which communication was needed) are ones that occupational therapy practitioners can use to elicit communication in the context of play.

Social Stories.™ Social Stories (Gray, 2000) are individualized stories written to guide a child's social behavior. Social Stories are read to the child with autism prior to an event to give him or her directives for expected behaviors. The stories describe events in the child's natural environment and target particular undesired behaviors that need to be modified. They also can target appropriate behaviors that are not consistently demonstrated and need to be reinforced. Social Stories present descriptive, directive, perspective, and affirmative statements related to the social situation at hand. The story instructs the child in what behaviors are expected for the coming activity and often include praise or reinforcement for positive behaviors. Occupational therapy practitioners frequently use Social Stories because they are individualized to the child and apply a positive, proactive method to encourage appropriate behavior. Social Stories are most effective when they are used consistently; therefore, the approach is typically adopted by the entire team, including the family.

Research evidence on Social Stories. Reynhout and Carter (2006) reviewed the empirical evidence on the effects of Social Stories in a systematic review that included 16 studies, 12 of which were single-subject design. The studies measured the targeted skills to determine intervention effectiveness. All but 4 studies demonstrated positive behavioral changes. Of the 12 studies with positive effects, 9 reported appropriate reduction in targeted behavior and 8 reported appropriate increases in targeted behaviors. Although Social Stories appear effective in changing social behaviors, the effects were small, partially because most of the trials have been single-subject studies (Reynhout & Carter, 2006).

Comprehensive behavioral interventions. Behavioral interventions that use applied behavioral analysis with discrete trial training are popular approaches for children with ASDs. Occupational therapists may provide intervention to children who receive intensive behavioral intervention and consult with the psychologists and behavioral therapists directing the behavioral program. Occupational therapy practitioners are rarely primary in the development of behavioral programs and are rarely primary in the implementation, which is generally accomplished by paraprofessionals trained in the specific methods. Although occupational therapy practitioners tend to be involved indirectly in intensive behavioral intervention, they should be knowledgeable

about the interventions to collaborate with the behavioral team and provide explanations to families about the programs.

Intensive behavioral intervention (discrete trial training). Intensive behavior intervention is currently defined as a home-based 30- to 40-hours per week discrete trial training program. It is typically implemented by four to six paraprofessionals (often students) who are trained and closely supervised. In some programs, parents and relatives participate in the training. The primary strategy of the program is highly structured, one-on-one, discrete trial training. Developmental appropriate goals are established and skill components are identified to be taught step-by-step. The skills are taught by presenting the task, allowing the child to respond to the instruction or to imitate the action, and reinforcing the child's response. The task and reinforcement are repeated for 3 to 8 trials to ensure that the child has mastered the skill. Skill mastery in discrete trials is defined as 90% accuracy across 2 days of intervention (Cohen, Amerine-Dickens, & Smith, 2006). Developmental skills across all domains are taught, with emphasis on language and cognitive skills, but including self-care skills and play competency.

Since the original discrete trial training designed by Lovaas (1987), the behavioral programs have been extended to include consultation with the early childhood staff or school personnel to implement the behavioral program in an environment outside the home. The phases that follow the home-based, 30–40 hours a week program are designed to help the child generalize his or her skills. The program systematically decreases the one-on-one treatment to enable the child to practice skills in a more natural environment (e.g., school).

Occupational therapy practitioners may provide intervention in addition to the behavioral program; however, it is important to consider the time demands of the intervention on the family. Practitioners should collaborate with the behavioral team to embed strategies or goals that reflect occupational therapy perspectives within the program. Occupational therapy practitioners offer valuable consultation to families who are considering a behavioral program for their child and can provide support and intervention to assist the child and family in transitioning from a home-based behavioral program to an interdisciplinary school-based one. Behavioral programs have become more interdisciplinary in many areas of the country, opening opportunities for leadership and participation by occupational therapists in the child's intervention program.

Research evidence on behavioral interventions. Behavioral interventions for children with autism have been well researched in the past 20 years. The original study of discrete trial training, published in 1987, described a nonrandomized trial by Lovaas. Based on a sample of 38, 19 children with autism (initial mean age = 34.6 months) received 40 hours per week of intensive discrete trial training and 19 children with autism (initial mean age = 40.9 months) received 10 or fewer hours per week of similar training. Each group received at least 2 years of treatment, and follow-up assessment was made when the children were age 7 years. Compared to the control group, the children who received the intensive behavioral treatment scored significantly higher in IQ. At the time of the posttest, 9 of the children who received behavioral treatment were in regular education and had IQs in the normal range, and 1 of the children in the control group was in regular education and had an IQ in the normal range.

A follow-up study by McEachie, Smith, and Lovaas (1993) evaluated this group of children between ages 3 and 6 years after the end of the first study. At this time, the mean age of the intensive behavioral treatment group was 13 years; the mean age of the control group (less-intense treatment) was 10 years (the control group entered the Lovaas study after the treatment group). The intensive treatment children had continued in treatment for an average of 5 years and had maintained the original positive results (i.e., 9 of 19 were in regular education and 11 demonstrated an IQ of at least 80). The control group had continued the less-intensive treatment for an average of 3 years and none were in regular education; 3 demonstrated an IQ of at least 80. The intensive treatment group scored significantly higher than the control group in IQ and

adaptive behaviors and lower in maladaptive behavior and psychotic personality traits. Therefore, McEachie and colleagues (1993) confirmed the original results of Lovaas (1987).

In 2000, Smith, Groen, and Wynn (who were trained by Lovaas) examined the effectiveness of discrete trial training with young children (n = 28, mean age = 36 months) diagnosed with PDD. In a randomized study, 15 children (12 boys, 3 girls) received intensive treatment for 30 hours per week over 18 months and were compared to a group of 13 children (11 boys, 2 girls) who received parental training 5 hours per week for 3 to 9 months. Parents were trained to use the same methods of discrete trial training and were asked to work with their children for 5 hours per week on the program. The children were assessed at ages 7 to 8 years. Those children who received the intensive-behavior treatment achieved significantly higher IQs, visual–spatial skills, and language development. Adaptive behaviors were no different in the two groups.

Cohen and colleagues (2006) also replicated the findings from the Lovaas studies using early intensive behavioral treatment (EIBT). In this 3-year prospective Level II study, 21 children received EIBT, and 21 who were age- and IQ-matched received community-based services (occupational, physical, speech–language, and some behavioral therapy for 5 hours per week). The children in EIBT received intensive services (35–40 hours/week), primarily in the home, for a year; they then received less-intense services emphasizing peer interaction in preschools; and finally, they moved to integrated models of services delivery that involved primarily consultation, environmental modification, and facilitation of peer interaction. At the end of year 3, the children in EIBT scored significantly higher in IQ, language comprehension, and adaptive behavior. They were not higher on other cognition measures and expressive language. Most (17 of 21) of the EIBT children were enrolled in a regular education classroom, and only 1 of the 21 children in the comparison group was in regular education. One reason for this significant difference in school placement was that integrating the children into regular education classrooms was a component of the EIBT. This study supported the positive effects of EIBT but did not find the dramatic effects reported in earlier studies (e.g., Lovaas, 1987).

The importance of using typical peers in behavioral interventions for children with autism was demonstrated by Smith, Lovaas, and Lovaas (2002) in a study that examined the effects of behavioral treatment when children were paired with typical peers compared to when they were paired with peers with developmental delays. This study demonstrated the evolution of discrete trial training from 40 hours of intensive training at home to an integrated, less intense training that can be implemented in inclusive preschool settings. In this nonrandomized trial, 9 children with autism were paired with a child who was developing typically for two sessions, then paired with a child with developmental delays for two sessions. They were videotaped and rated on five different behaviors. The children demonstrated more interactive play and speech in the condition with a peer who was developing typically. They also displayed less self-stimulation but did not differ in solitary play. Occupational therapy practitioners often provide services in small groups; these findings suggest that when peers who are developing typically are selected for the groups, interaction and language may increase.

Sallows and Graupner (2005) examined whether a community-based program in which parents were taught to implement discrete trial training could produce the same results as a therapist-directed clinic-based treatment. Using a randomized controlled trial, a clinic-based, therapist-directed group of 13 children (11 boys, 2 girls) with autism was compared to a parent-directed group of 10 children (8 boys, 2 girls). The clinic-based group received 40 hours a week of discrete trial training, and the parent-directed group, who received therapist consultation, averaged 32 hours of home-based intervention. After 4 years of treatment, the children in both groups improved 25 points in IQ, and cognitive performance, language, adaptive behavior, and social behavior outcomes for the two groups were similar. Both intensive interventions resulted in clinically significant changes, suggesting that parent-mediated intervention can be as effective as therapist-

directed sessions. Children with greater imitation, language, and social responsiveness initially made the greatest gains.

Luiselli, Cannon, Ellis, and Sisson (2000) evaluated the effects of home-based intensive behavioral treatment using a retrospective analysis. This analysis examined the outcomes of 16 children to determine if those who started intervention at a younger age (before 3 years) achieved better outcomes. It also examined how duration and intensity of treatment influenced outcomes. These researchers found that the age at which treatment began and the intensity of the treatment did not influence outcomes; however, duration of the treatment predicted children's improvement in communication, cognition, and social–emotional domains. This study counters claims that behavioral treatment must begin before 3 years and supports a longer duration of treatment.

Eldevik, Eikeseth, Jahr, and Smith (2006) also investigated behavioral treatment using discrete trial training at lower intensity than was originally researched by Lovaas (1987). This research team from Norway retrospectively compared children who had received low-intensity behavioral treatment (12.5 hours/week for 20 months) to children who received a comparable amount of eclectic treatment (12 hours/week for 20 months). A group of 13 (10 boys, 3 girls) with autism and mental retardation who received behavioral treatment was compared to a group of 15 (14 boys,1 girl) who received eclectic treatment (e.g., alternative communication, sensorimotor therapies). The children who received the behavioral treatment made significantly greater gains in intellectual functioning, language, and communication. The groups did not differ in daily living skills or adaptive behavior. These studies suggest that discrete trial training can produce positive effects when implemented in a more integrated way and on a less-intense schedule than originally proposed by Lovaas. Performance gains with behavioral treatments, however, may not include adaptive behaviors.

Positive behavioral support. Positive behavioral support intervention is widely implemented and has a strong base of research supporting its effectiveness (U.S. OSEP, n.d.). Because this type of intervention is based on an individual analysis of the child's behavior to determine the underlying causes for the behavior and is implemented in the natural environment, occupational therapists frequently design and use this intervention. The goal of positive behavioral support is to prevent problem behaviors, and its pivotal element is functional assessment. In functional assessment, the team analyzes the underlying cause of the problem behavior to determine why it occurred and what is reinforcing the behavior. The activities that occurred prior to the behavior and the consequences of the behavior are evaluated to determine how these influence repetition of the behavior. Once the team determines the antecedents to a problem behavior, they design strategies to combat it, such as modifying the environment, the child's schedule, or the classroom activities. Similar to occupational therapy approaches, the goal is to design an environment that matches the child's behaviors. When the demands placed on the child are consistent with the child's capabilities, he or she no longer needs to use problem behaviors.

Positive behavioral support is a comprehensive intervention that includes (1) using the functional assessment to identify causative factors, (2) incorporating multiple behavioral interventions throughout the day, and (3) consistently applying the procedures developed by the team (Horner, Carr, Strain, Todd, & Reed, 2002). Targeted behaviors include aggression toward others, self-injury, tantrums, and disruptive behaviors. A wide range of behavioral approaches are used, depending on how the child responds and what is most appropriate to the problem and the setting. Horner and colleagues listed five common procedures applied with children with autism, all based in behavioral theory: (1) stimulus based (altering the antecedent), (2) instruction based (direct instruction regarding appropriate behavior), (3) extinction based (withholding or minimizing delivery of reinforcers), (4) reinforcement based (rewards to increase behaviors), and (5) punishment based (may be positive or negative). The team decides which of these procedures to use and in which context and activity they should be imple-

mented. These procedures need to be implemented consistently by all adults who interact with the child to be optimally effective.

Research evidence on positive behavioral support. Horner and colleagues (2002) examined the effectiveness of positive behavioral support interventions on reducing problem behaviors. Their systematic review analyzed the findings of five review papers and nine studies of positive behavioral support with children with autism. Of the 37 comparisons in these studies, the child's tantrums decreased 85% of the time. In 59% of the comparisons, problem behaviors were reduced by at least 90%. Horner and colleagues concluded that early use of behavioral interventions can result in reductions of problem behaviors by 80% to 90%. The researchers consistently found that successful interventions were developed from a functional assessment that identified the antecedents and consequences to the child's behavior. This systematic review provides very strong evidence for the effectiveness of positive behavioral interventions.

Overall Themes From the Research Evidence

When the studies on interventions for children with autism are examined together, certain characteristics of intervention are consistently linked to positive outcomes. This section summarizes the themes that ran through many of the studies and defines the critical aspects of effective intervention for children with autism. The themes that emerged from the research evidence are as follows:

1. Effective intervention programs are developed from individualized analysis that includes assessment of the physiological basis for behaviors and the environment's influence on behavior;
2. The child's family is central to the intervention program and services should include family support and education;
3. Intervention services need to be intensive and comprehensive; and
4. Facilitating active engagement of the child is the essential priority for all interventions.

Each theme is expanded in the section below.

Individualized analysis of the child. Although ASDs are defined as a set of characteristics, these characteristics manifest in unique ways for each child. ASDs are pervasive; however, they seldom result in global developmental delays. Instead, the child with an ASD often presents with performance strengths and limitations, showing a scattering of skills (with certain skills at or even above the child's chronological age level and others well below). Adaptive behaviors are difficult to categorize or predict, ranging from very appropriate behaviors, extremely passive or nonresponsive, to disruptive temper tantrums or irrational aggression. The individualized and sometimes complex presentation suggests that in-depth evaluation across all occupational performance areas is essential to guide successful intervention.

Comprehensive evaluation of children with an ASD also includes assessment of the physiological basis for behaviors. Most individuals with an ASD have sensory processing problems (e.g., hypo- or hypersensitivity). Sensory processing disorders can influence the child's arousal level, attention span, and social interaction. These disorders can also relate to the stereotypic behaviors (e.g., hand flapping, rocking) they exhibit. Evaluation that identifies how sensory processing influences behaviors enables professionals to develop strategies that support the child's sensory needs.

In recognition of the pervasive nature of ASDs, most of the intervention trials used a comprehensive battery of tests to plan the intervention and measure its effects. A comprehensive evaluation captures the individualized profile of the child and helps to identify causative factors, as well as performance levels. Occupational therapists contribute to assessment of children with ASDs by evaluating across performance domains (e.g., cognition, fine motor, play, social interaction). Therapists also take a leadership role in analysis of behavior by providing specific assessment of the underlying physiological functions, such as sensory processing, motor planning, arousal, attention, and muscle tone, that influence the child's behavior.

Family is central. The importance of holding the family as central to the intervention program for their children is well established (Dunst, Hamby, Trivett, Raab, & Bruder, 2000; Turnbull, Turbiville, & Turnbull, 2000). Studies of autism intervention recognize the importance of embracing the parents and other family members when designing intervention services for children.

Although professionals agree that families need to be involved in the child's program, the research literature prescribes different meanings to family-centered intervention. In several studies, the researchers taught the parents to implement the intervention. Sallows and Graupner (2005) examined the effects of directing parents to provide 32 hours of behavioral interventions in their homes. The parent-directed therapy program was as effective as behavioral interventions provided by clinicians. In a comparative study of social intervention, researchers taught parents two different interventions and compared the effects on parent–child interaction (Koegel, Bimbela, & Schreibman, 1996). The parents were more motivated and less stressed by the intervention using naturally occurring events and reinforcers compared to teaching discrete skills outside the natural context.

Other researchers provided parent education to help parents gain understanding of their child's behavior and increase their skills in managing behaviors. Sofronoff and Farbotko (2002) and Sofronoff, Leslie, and Brown (2004) organized workshops on parent management of problem behaviors in children with Asperger syndrome. The training resulted in reduction of problem behaviors and an increase in parents' confidence. Other studies have reported that parent education is empowering and viewed as helpful by parents (e.g., Jocelyn, Casiro, Beattie, Bow, & Kneisz, 1998; Panerai et al., 2002). As summarized in a 2006 Cochrane review (Diggle, McConachie, & Randle, 2006), Jocelyn and colleagues (1998) randomly assigned 35 preschool children with a diagnosis of autism or pervasive developmental disorder to an experimental or control group. Children in the experimental group were enrolled in day care, and a 12-week intervention consisting of lectures and on-site consultations at day care centers was provided to the parents and child care workers. Additional family support (e.g., lectures, on-site consultations) was also provided. Control participants received only day care. In the experimental group, children showed greater gains in language abilities, and the caregivers demonstrated significant increases in knowledge about autism, greater perception of control, and greater parent satisfaction.

Several studies included parent support and opportunities for networking and discussion with other parents as a component of the intervention. In LeGoff (2004), parents met separately while their children participated in the Lego groups. These parent groups offered information and provided opportunities for informal discussions. LeGoff believed that the parent networking contributed to the success of the intervention but did not directly measure the effects.

In relationship-based intervention (e.g., Greenspan & Wieder, 1997; Mahoney & Perales, 2005), the parents' relationship with their child is the focus of the intervention program. The therapist teaches the parents strategies for playing with and imitating the child to facilitate increased social interaction and responsiveness. These interventions that directly support the parent–child relationship validate that the family is the most essential aspect of the child's development.

With these differing views of the family's role, the definition of family-centered intervention becomes somewhat blurred. A consistent theme is the importance of family education about autism, resources, and intervention strategies. Parental satisfaction increases when information and education about the disability, resources, and interventions is provided (e.g., Turnbull et al., 2000). Educational interventions that increase parents' skills in managing behaviors also reduce stress and increase confidence (Sofronoff et al., 2004). Interventions that focus on the parent–child relationship and facilitate high-quality interactions within naturally occurring routines appear to improve relationships, increase developmental skills, and result in family satisfaction with services (Greenspan & Wieder, 1997;

Mahoney & Perales, 2005; Wieder & Greenspan, 2005). Interventions that require parents to implement behavioral techniques (Sallows & Graupner, 2005) and teach the child specific skills (Panerai et al., 2002) can be stressful for parents. When parents are placed in the role of teacher for large portions of the day, they may not feel that they are adequately performing their roles as parents.

Although the studies do not have consensus on how families should participate in intervention programs, the vital nature of their roles is a consistent thread among the studies. Because families know their child best and spend the greatest amount of time with them, they are the essential element in creating and sustaining a nurturing environment in which the child can grow and develop. This implies that occupational therapy practitioners always should provide families with information, support, and resources. Occupational therapy services that are of greatest benefit to the child embrace the family's priorities and concerns.

Intensive and comprehensive services. The studies with greatest positive effects on the children's performance were provided on an intensive schedule over an extended period (e.g., Cohen et al., 2006; Greenspan & Wieder, 1997; Lovaas, 1987). The interventions with greatest effects were also comprehensive and designed to meet the multiple needs of these children across domains (e.g., Greenspan & Wieder, 1997; Rogers & DiLalla, 1991). Although this theme seems both logical and obvious, the need for intensive intervention for children with autism is particularly critical to successful outcomes. Early intensive behavioral interventions produced moderate to strong effects when provided 32 to 40 hours per week for 1 to 2 years (Smith et al., 2000). DIR or floortime intervention also resulted in substantial improvements in children's functioning when provided on a rigorous twice-a-day schedule (Wieder & Greenspan, 2005).

Similarly, in another controlled treatment study incorporating a child-led approach, an intensive 1:1 treatment program (Salt et al., 2001) targeting social-communication and play skill development yielded significantly improved measures of joint attention, social interaction, imitation, daily living skills, motor skills, and adaptive behavior in the treatment group when compared to controls (Salt et al., 2002). Because children with autism easily become disengaged when they are not guided in a focused learning experience, they have limited ability to learn outside the context of intervention. Without direct support to engage in and to attend to the activity, a child with autism may demonstrate nonpurposeful actions or disengaged behaviors. With limited self-initiated learning, a child with an ASD needs intensive programming throughout much of the day. This programming should be consistent and comprehensive and should be based on the individualized analysis of the child's performance and behavior.

Another aspect of intensity that bears highlighting is the importance of a low child-to-interventionist ratio (Myers et al., 2007; National Research Council, 2001). A low student-to-adult ratio is a key element of many of the interventions yielding favorable outcomes. In educational programs (e.g., TEACCH), a low student-to-adult ratio allows for adequate periods of that one-on-one and small-group instruction that is necessary in these individualized, comprehensive programs. Within a behavioral intervention program (e.g., Lovaas, 1987; Smith et al., 2000), the 1:1 programming allows for consistent responding to and reinforcement of behavior. Similarly, when implementing an intervention based on DIR or floortime, the individualized nature of the intervention affords the interventionist the ability to scaffold during the child-directed activities to promote attainment of outcomes (Wieder & Greenspan, 2005).

Although the research demonstrates the importance of intensive intervention, practice models do not always offer intensive programming. Service delivery models affordable to families that accommodate the competing demands on professionals need to be developed. Creative use of paraprofessional and consultation models is needed to respond to the growing need for intensive service with this population.

Engagement. Actively engaging children with autism in the intervention programs must also be viewed as a common theme, as it underlies comprehensive, intensive, individualized, family-centered programs. Further, this emphasis on engagement is germane to occupational therapy intervention, as "promoting the health and participation of people, organizations, and populations through engagement in occupation" is the primary target outcome of the occupational therapy process (AOTA, 2008b, p. 626). Here, engagement is "the commitment made to performance in occupations as the result of choice, motivation, and meaning and includes the objective and subjective aspects of carrying out activities meaningful and purposeful to the individual person, organization, or population" (AOTA, 2008b, p. 660).

The importance of facilitating active engagement in educating children with an ASD is well documented in the literature. The U. S. Department of Education, Office of Special Education Programs, National Research Council formed the Committee on Educational Interventions for Children with Autism (National Research Council, 2001) and charged the committee to integrate scientific, theoretical, and policy literature and create a framework for evaluating scientific evidence concerning the features and effects of educational programming for young children with autism. The primary focus of the charge was to define the effective programs for children ages 8 years or younger with autism. In analyzing the conclusions and recommendations drawn by this council relating to both the goals of educational programs and characteristics of effective programs, it becomes clear that individualized educational programming for young children with autism promotes active engagement (National Research Council, 2001).

This view is supported by several other reviews and analyses of effective programs for individuals with autism (Bryson, Rogers, & Fombonne, 2003; Dawson & Osterling, 1997; Dunlap, 1999; Hurth, Shaw, Izeman, Whaley, & Rogers, 1999; Strain, Wolery, & Izeman, 1998) and can be seen as an integral component of many of the interventions reviewed above. Active engagement is a component of various treatment approaches, including discrete trial training (Lovaas, 1987; Smith et al., 2000), incidental teaching (McGee, Morrier, & Daly, 1999), and structured teaching (McGee et al., 1999; Schopler, Mesibov, & Hearsey, 1995), that have shown effectiveness.

A key component to the active engagement construct is the ability to sustain attention of an activity or person (de Kruif & McWilliam, 1999; McWilliam & Bailey, 1992). Active engagement is a qualitative construct that includes the focus and level of engagement (e.g., pretend play, attention, persistence, participation, undifferentiated behavior). Engagement goes beyond measurement of the amount of time a child spends in an activity to capture important behaviors for learning (de Kruif & McWilliam, 1999), such as the child's motivation for mastery and the extent of goal-directed behavior. Active engagement is a stable construct that appears to be related to internal child factors (temperament or diagnosis), observable child behaviors (level of play skill), and environmental factors (type of classroom activity; de Kruif & McWilliam, 1999; McWilliam & Bailey, 1992; McWilliam, Trivette, & Dunst, 1985).

Researchers also have identified relationships between child engagement and environmental variables, including physical (e.g., structured teaching materials, visual supports) and social supports (e.g., peer models) and types of instructional strategies. Specific to autism, most researchers have evaluated the effects of instructional and social language strategies on engagement. Readers are encouraged to read Ruble and Robson (2007) for a comprehensive review of these works.

The effect of sensory processing deficits in children with autism on learning and engagement has not been studied. Children who are auditorily, visually, tactilely, taste/smell, and/or movement sensitive may seek sensory input or appear distractible as they seek to avoid sensory input in the environment, whereas others may be hyporesponsive and passive as they fail to orient and respond to typical levels of sensory input in the environment (Dunn, 1997; Miller & Lane, 2000; Miller & Summers, 2001). A child with a sensory modulation deficit experiences a mismatch between the external contextual demands of his or her environment and his or her internal characteristics (e.g., attention, emotion, sensory processing; Miller, Reisman, McIntosh, & Simon, 2001) that impairs his or her ability to sustain active engagement with people or the activity at hand. Recognizing the impact of the sensory environment reduces the degree to which skill development rests solely on internal child factors and guides parents, teachers, and practitioners to effective environmental strategies that can improve child engagement and yield optimal outcomes (Reinhartsen, Garfinkle, & Wolery, 2002; Ruble & Dalrymple, 1996, 2002; Wolery, 2000; Wolery & Garfinkle, 2002).

When considered together, these intervention themes become foundation components in the development of intervention plans and are important considerations when evaluating existing programs of a child. The actual implementation and utilization of these themes vary and can be dependent on the setting and context of the intervention program. Table 8 summarizes some potential applications.

Recommendations for Practice

On the basis of the overall themes that emerged from the synthesis of research studies, the following practice recommendations are made:

Evaluation

- In addition to evaluating the child's performance in all areas of occupation, the occupational therapy evaluation of the child should include analysis of the physiological functions that may influence the child's behaviors (e.g., sensory processing disorders, sleep disorders).
- Evaluation of the child with an ASD should include assessment of the environment's influence on behavior.

Intervention

- Regardless of the setting, occupational therapy intervention should be intensive (e.g., one-on-one, intensive time commitment, daily intervention). Both direct and consultative services are important. The occupational therapist's consultation should emphasize the individuals who interact with the child on a frequent basis.
- Given the pervasive nature of ASDs, occupational therapy services should be comprehensive (i.e., should address self-care, work, educational, and play occupations). They should also include underlying sensorimotor issues that relate to the child's performance and behavior. Intervention needs to focus on inhibiting certain behaviors that disrupt participation, such as on temper tantrums or inappropriate behaviors, as well as on facilitating self-regulation and performance that increases participation.
- Given the profile of children with an ASD, the focus of occupational therapy should be on facilitating active engagement of the child. Active engagement includes appropriate attention and arousal, sustained eye contact, joint attention to an activity and another person, appropriate affect, communication of needs, turn taking, gesturing as part of interaction, and initiation of social engagement.

Centrality of the Family

- Occupational therapy practitioners should acknowledge that the family is the decision maker for the child and needs to be fully informed about resources and systems.
- Occupational therapy services should support the family by listening, showing empathy, discussing the child in sensitive ways, educating the family about the disability, advocating for them, and promoting self-advocacy.
- Occupational therapy practitioners should give families information and guidance to enhance their child's participation across environments.

■ ■ ■

Table 8. Application of the Guidelines: Examples of Evaluation and Intervention

Description of Client	Evaluation	Intervention
	▪ Is comprehensive, assessing performance across occupations ▪ Includes interview, structured observation, and standardized testing ▪ Includes analysis of behavior with an emphasis on how sensory processing and the environment influence behavior	▪ Is intensive and comprehensive ▪ Emphasizes social engagement and participation ▪ Includes strategies to decrease behaviors that interfere with performance ▪ Emphasizes family priorities
▪ Justin is a 5-year-old boy with moderately high-functioning autism. ▪ He is in kindergarten and presents with behavior regulation difficulties and social communication deficits. ▪ He demonstrates minimal social initiation and diminished social responding, especially with peers. ▪ When peers initiate interaction and he does respond, he often does so aggressively.	▪ Structured clinical observations of behavior, social communication, parent–child interaction, and play skills ▪ *Short Sensory Profile* (McIntosh et al., 1999) ▪ *School Function Assessment* (cognitive–behavior scales; Coster et al., 1998) ▪ Functional analysis of aggressive behaviors	▪ Based on the functional analysis of aggressive behaviors, a sensory diet is implemented to assist Justin with regulating his behavior. ▪ Additionally, Social Stories (Reynhout & Carter, 2006) are used prior to challenging school situations (e.g., standing in line, assemblies, fire drills) to coach appropriate behavior. ▪ Peer buddies and modeling are used to build social communication skills during naturally reinforcing play activities. ▪ Ongoing consultation with the classroom teacher and family allow for generalization of strategies across home and school settings.
▪ Ryan is a 4-year-old boy with low-functioning autism. ▪ He presents with poor self-regulation, behavior problems (e.g., frequent tantrums, screaming), and a lack of purposeful play. ▪ Ryan uses behavior rather than spoken language to communicate. ▪ He attends a comprehensive preschool classroom of children with and without disabilities.	▪ Clinical observations of behavior, self-regulation, parent–child interaction, parenting strategies, and play skills ▪ *Sensory Profile* (Dunn, 1999)	▪ OT services are provided weekly in a clinical setting with the parent present and consultation with Ryan's preschool team. ▪ Services focus on improving self-regulation to allow for socially appropriate behavior (Greenspan & Wieder, 1997; Mahoney & Perales, 2005). ▪ Strategies include sensory integration techniques (Baranek, 2002), visual supports for structure (Ozonoff & Cathcart, 1998) and communication and behavioral strategies, including positive reinforcement. Behavioral strategies include redirection, elimination of antecedents to his tantrums, and reinforcing his positive behaviors (Horner et al., 2002). ▪ Parent education includes positive behavioral support strategies and visual aids for communication. ▪ The OT helps Ryan's parents recognize when Ryan is becoming overaroused and implement sensory strategies to help him modulate his arousal (Baranek, 2002).

(continued)

Table 8. Application of the Guidelines: Examples of Evaluation and Intervention (cont.)

Description of Client	Evaluation	Intervention
▪ Michael is a 3-year-old boy with moderate autism. ▪ His mother's primary concerns are his limited social interaction, delayed pretend play, hyperactive behaviors, and picky eating. ▪ Michael also is receiving speech therapy services at the clinic and an Applied Behavioral Analysis program at home.	▪ Clinical observations of behavior during free play, self-regulation, and parent–child interaction during play ▪ Structured observation of parent–child interaction while Michael is eating ▪ *Sensory Profile* (Dunn, 1999) ▪ *Bayley Scales of Infant Development* (cognitive, fine motor, social–emotional, adaptive behavior scales; Bayley, 2005) ▪ *Pediatric Evaluation of Disability Inventory, Self-Care Scale* (Haley et al., 1992)	▪ OT services are provided weekly in a clinical setting with the parent present. ▪ Services address self-regulation, social engagement, and pretend play skills (Greenspan & Wieder, 1997; Mahoney & Perales, 2005). OT intervention includes behavioral strategies to improve eating (Horner et al., 2002). ▪ Intervention methods include sensory integration techniques; behavioral strategies, including positive reinforcement; and reciprocal play to improve social interaction. ▪ The OT and speech–language pathologist communicate weekly regarding Michael's intervention program and arrange cotreatment sessions. ▪ The behavioral therapist (Cohen et al., 2006; Smith et al., 2000) attends some OT sessions to observe and learn sensory strategies helpful in modulating Michael's behavior. ▪ Parent training includes information on sensory processing and behavior management strategies (Koegel et al., 1996). ▪ The OT provides parent consultation to improve the family's mealtime routine and to increase the variety of foods Michael eats.
• Shari is a 9-year-old girl with moderate-functioning autism. • Her family brings her to OT to assist them in promoting functional independence. • Shari does not demonstrate significant behavior management difficulties. Instead, she is described as somewhat passive and difficult to motivate to stay on tasks until they are completed. • She requires significant prompting and assistance for ADL and IADL in the home.	• Occupational profile conducted with Shari's family to identify need areas and priorities • Structured clinical observations of motor performance, behavior, social communication, parent–child interaction, and play skills • *Vineland Adaptive Behavior Scales* (Sparrow et al., 1984) • *Sensory Profile* (Dunn, 1999)	▪ OT clinical services are provided weekly with the parents present. Once a month, the OT makes a home visit. This collaborative intervention model promotes similar structure and activities across environments (Cohen et al., 2006). ▪ Intervention initially focused on foundational performance skills (i.e., motor planning and sequencing) related to the ADL and independent-living skills prioritized by the family. ▪ Task analysis visual supports were used to assist Shari with sustained attention for and sequencing of ADL tasks (Koegel et al., 1996). ▪ The OT emphasized use of the phone and strategies to promote Shari's safety, working toward the goal that she could be left alone at home for short periods. ▪ A self-monitoring picture schedule was used to facilitate independence across environments (Panerai et al., 2002). ▪ Parents were encouraged to routinely use visual cueing methods and visual supports to promote Shari's independence in ADLs and household tasks (Panerai et al., 2002).

Case Description	Assessment	Intervention
■ Marla is an 18-year-old young woman with moderate autism. She lives in a group home that provides 24-hour supervision. ■ Care and therapeutic services are provided through the Department of Developmental Disabilities. ■ Marla verbalizes her basic needs; however, her speech is rapid and difficult to decipher. ■ Marla becomes anxious when her routine is disturbed, demands are placed on her, or her desires are not granted. ■ She has poor behavioral and emotional regulation that often results in aggressive behavior toward self or others.	■ Occupational profile is assessed through interview ■ Adaptive behavior scales ■ Clinical observations of behavior in social situations, cognitive processing during a multistep task ■ *Canadian Occupational Performance Measure* (Law et al., 1994)	■ OT intervention services are provided for Marla weekly in the group home setting. ■ The OT teaches her sensory strategies to modulate arousal (Baranek, 2002), structures tasks into small steps using visual schedules and visual aids (Reynhout & Carter, 2006), and uses cognitive–behavioral strategies to reduce her anxiety (Bauminger, 2002). ■ Educational strategies, such as forward and backward chaining, visual supports, and environmental structure, are implemented to support success during intervention (Horner et al., 2002; Hwang & Hughes, 2000) and during everyday activities. ■ OT services address individual skill development, staff training, environmental accommodations, and environmental supports. ■ OT focused on the family's priorities to improve Shari's ADL, IADL, and social participation.
■ E.J. is a 20-year-old young man with Asperger syndrome. E.J. is currently in his senior year of high school and is having difficulty finding a job. ■ He lives independently in an apartment. ■ He presents with poor grooming and hygiene skills and pragmatic language deficits. ■ He has several interests but spends most of his free time reading about antique cars.	■ Interview about his concerns and interests ■ Structured observation of role-playing a job interview ■ *Scales of Independent Behavior–Revised* (Bruininks et al., 1997)	■ OT clinical services are initially provided weekly in the clinic, then in the community. ■ Services initially address grooming and hygiene needs through the use of a very specific step-by-step self-monitoring system. ■ Consultation with the Division of Vocational Rehabilitation was initiated to assist in the employment search. ■ Role-playing, video self-modeling, and collaborative problem solving were used to address social communication/pragmatic language needs relating to the interview process and interaction with coworkers. ■ Job coaching was used to allow E.J. to learn and master job functions and to problem solve when needed.

Source: Adapted from Watling, R., Tomchek, S., & LaVesser, P. (2005). The scope of occupational therapy services for individuals with autism spectrum disorders across the lifespan. *American Journal of Occupational Therapy, 59,* 680–683.

Note. ADLs = activities of daily living. IADLs = instrumental activities of daily living. OT = occupational therapy or occupational therapist.

Appendix A. Motor Performance and Sensory Processing in Children With an ASD

Postural Control and Gross Motor Functioning

Historically, *postural control* and *gross motor functioning* has been studied in the context of developmental milestones (DeMyer, Hingtgen, & Jackson, 1981; Losche, 1990; Wing, 1972) and/or gait (Hallett et al., 1993; Kohen-Raz, Volkmar, & Cohen, 1992; Maurer & Damasio, 1982; Vilensky, Damasio, & Maurer, 1981). In comparison to language and social skills, individuals with an ASD have been described as having better basic motor skills (Klin, Volkmar, & Sparrow, 1992; Wing, 1972). The timing and sequence of motor developmental markers, however, have been described as both delayed and qualitatively different in individuals with ASDs than those of typically developing children (Losche, 1990). Hypotonia also has been frequently reported in individuals with autism (Bauman, 1999; Haas et al., 1996; Rapin, 1996), although in at least one study no differences were noted when tone was compared to mental-age-matched typically developing children (Jones & Prior, 1985). Postural and movement abnormalities, along with general clumsiness, have been a frequent finding (DeMyer, 1976; Ghaziuddin, Tsai, & Ghaziuddin, 1992; Jones & Prior, 1985; Klin, Volkmar, Sparrow, Cicchetti, & Rourke, 1995; Leary & Hill, 1996; Nass & Gutman, 1997). Gait disturbances, including toe walking and arching of the trunk (Eisenmajer et al., 1996; Haas et al., 1996; Hallett et al., 1993; Kohen-Raz et al., 1992; Vilensky et al., 1981), have been noted, although some studies have reported no group differences in gait beyond that accounted for by cognitive level (Jones & Prior, 1985; Rapin, 1996). Balance and vestibular-responding deficits also were often reported. In some studies these deficits have been linked to impairments in visually perceiving environmental motion (Gepner & Mestre, 2002; Gepner, Mestre, Masson, & de Schonen, 1995). Ball play deficits also have been reported in children with ASDs (Manjiviona & Prior, 1995; Miyahara et al., 1997).

Handedness

Initial studies relating to fine motor skill often focused on *handedness*. A high prevalence (approximately 40%) of ambiguous or inconsistent handedness has been reported in individuals with autism (Fein, Humes, Kaplan, Lucci, & Waterhouse, 1984; Hauck & Dewey, 2001; McManus, Murray, Doyle, & Baron-Cohen, 1982; Satz, Green, & Lyon, 1989; Satz, Soper, Orsini, Henry, & Zvi, 1985; Soper et al., 1986), in contrast to rates of the typically developing population (approximately 4%; Gudmundson, 1993). An increased prevalence of left-handedness in individuals with autism (approximately 15%–20%), when compared to children who are developing normally (approximately 9%), also has been reported in the literature (Fein et al., 1984; Hauck & Dewey, 2001; McManus et al., 1982; Satz et al., 1989; Soper et al., 1986).

Fine Motor Task Performance

When engaged in *fine motor task performance*, individuals with ASDs have demonstrated manual dexterity deficits on standardized measures (Hughes, 1996; Manjiviona & Prior, 1995; Mari, Castiello, Marks, Marraffa, & Prior, 2003; Miyahara et al., 1997; Provost, Heimerl, & Lopez, 2007; Provost, Lopez, & Heimerl, 2006). Further, while several investigations have reported slower speeds for timed pegboard completion (Cornish & McManus, 1996; Minshew, Goldstein, & Siegel, 1997; Rumsey & Hamburger, 1990; Szatmari, Tuff, Finlayson, & Bartolucci, 1990), others have reported no group differences (Ghaziuddin et al., 1992; McEvoy, Rogers, & Pennington, 1993). Motor learning also has been implicated, as increased difficulty with learning self-care and graphomotor tasks has been described in the literature (Szatmari, Bartolucci, & Bremner, 1989; Szatmari et al., 1990). Better performance by children with autism on goal-directed motor performance (e.g., reach, grasp, placing activities) has been noted in purposeful contexts in daily routines than in nonpurposeful conditions (Hughes & Russell, 1993; Rogers, Bennetto, McEvoy, & Pennington 1996).

Praxis

Praxis most often has been investigated within the framework of motor imitation studies and been found to be impaired in the majority of children with autism. In one large longitudinal study, imitation impairments were noted in more than 60% of the cohort (Rapin, 1996). Many investigative studies of praxis in children with autism have focused on motor imitation of body movements, facial expressions, gestures, and/or motor tasks (Dawson, Meltzoff, Osterling, & Rinaldi, 1998; Jones & Prior, 1985; Ohta, 1987; Rogers et al., 1996; Stone & Lemanek, 1990; Stone et al., 1990). When investigating motor imitation of hand and arm movements, individuals with autism performed more poorly

than cognitively matched controls, and often only partially responded to modeled motor actions (Charman, Swettenham, & Baron-Cohen, 1997; Jones & Prior, 1985; Ohta, 1987). Oral–motor praxis deficits, including poor range of movement, isolation of movement, and impaired execution of movement, were noted in children with autism following verbal and imitative prompts (Adams, 1998; Rapin, 1996). Similarly, Rogers and colleagues (1996) noted that individuals with autism demonstrated deficits in motor imitation on pantomime tasks using hand and facial movements. Stone and colleagues (1990) also analyzed imitation abilities for 12 motor tasks. Performance of 22 children with autism was compared to the performance of groups of children with mental retardation ($n = 15$), hearing impairments ($n = 15$), and language impairments ($n = 19$), and children who had no disability ($n = 20$). Imitation skills of the children with autism were significantly lower than those of the children in all the other groups and were reported to be the most important characteristic differentiating the children with autism from the others.

In another study investigating neuropsychological correlates of six early diagnostic symptoms in autism (Dawson et al., 1998), imitation abilities of young children with autism were compared to those of developmentally matched groups of children with Down syndrome or typical development. Here, analysis of both immediate and delayed imitation abilities involved a range of tasks, including gestures that the subjects could see themselves perform (e.g., hand opening and closing), those that they could not see themselves perform (e.g., eye blinking, mouth postures), novel acts (e.g., touching elbow to a panel), and familiar acts (e.g., banging blocks). In the immediate imitation condition, the children imitated a gestural model, whereas in the delayed imitation, the children were given a 10-minute interval during which to respond when the tasks with objects were modeled. Performance of the children with autism was significantly poorer than that of the other two groups for both immediate and delayed imitation tasks. Of the six autism symptoms evaluated (social orienting, immediate imitation, delayed imitation, shared attention, response to distress, and symbolic play), only the immediate imitation domain was significantly related to the severity of autism symptoms.

Several authors have theorized about and investigated factors affecting praxis. When evaluating task context, individuals with autism have had better performance and praxis for tasks with a purposeful context than for tasks with nonpurposeful contexts (Hughes & Russell, 1993; Rogers et al., 1996; Stone, Ousley, Yoder, Hogan, & Hepburn, 1997). Several studies have investigated the impact of task complexity on motor planning. In at least one study (Minshew et al., 1997), individuals with autism were reported to have intact motor planning for simple motor tasks but impaired praxis for complex motor tasks. Several other authors have described similar patterns and theorized that the difficulties with performance of complex motor tasks instead may reflect diminished ability to use external visual feedback that affects postural control, quality of movement, and motor sequencing (Bennetto, Pennington, & Rogers, 1996; Kohen-Raz et al., 1992; Smith & Bryson, 1998; Stone et al., 1990). Similarly, Dawson and Lew (1989), in an early theory formulation of autism etiology, proposed that the complex information processing demands inherent in social situations exceed the capabilities of young children with autism, leading to impaired capacity to engage in social exchanges (including imitation).

Only one study found attempted to differentiate between the praxis (movement preparation) and movement quality (movement execution) components of a motor task (Rinehart, Bradshaw, Brereton, & Tonge, 2001). In this study, movement preparation and execution were measured during a simple motor reprogramming task utilizing an odd-ball paradigm. This paradigm is often used in attention research and measures differences in the subject responding to a target condition randomly presented with similar stimuli. Results indicated that high-functioning children with autism ages 5 to 19 years had intact movement execution but atypical movement preparation when compared with typically developing, cognitively matched control children. More specifically, the children with autism demonstrated a lack of anticipation during movement

preparation phases and therefore required more time to respond. The authors questioned if both motivation and attention factors (i.e., sustained attention, shifting attention/executive function) may have confounded the results, thus mimicking decreased task preparation.

Children and adolescents with an ASD also respond to sensory experiences differently than peers without disabilities. These *sensory processing disorders* have been well documented in the basic science literature (Lincoln, Courchesne, Harms, & Allen, 1995; Ornitz, 1989; Ornitz, Lane, Sugiyama, & de Traversay, 1993; Yeung-Courchesne & Courchesne, 1997), clinical literature (Dawson & Watling, 2000; Ermer & Dunn, 1998; Kientz & Dunn, 1997; Watling, Deitz, & White, 2001), and first-person accounts of living with autism (Cesaroni & Garber, 1991; Grandin, 1992; Williams, 1995). In fact, the initial appearance of these sensory processing findings often predates diagnosis (Adrien et al., 1993; Baranek, 1999; Dahlgren & Gillberg, 1989; Lord, 1995).

The majority of research describing sensory processing disorders stems from parental reports, retrospective videotape analysis, and firsthand accounts of living with autism. Findings are organized into studies reporting sensory responding and modulation impairments (including firsthand accounts and descriptive studies of sensory processing) and studies using sensory processing as a discriminative function between children with autism and those with other developmental disorders. Note, this review will be limited to studies describing observable behaviors indicative of sensory processing patterns and does not include studies investigating neurophysiological processes.

Differences in Sensory Responding

Impairments with modulating incoming sensory input have been reported widely in the literature describing autism characteristics (Adrien, Ornitz, Barthelemy, Sauvage, & Lelord, 1987; Adrien et al., 1992, 1993; Baranek, 1999; Dahlgren & Gillberg, 1989; Kientz & Dunn, 1997; Ornitz, 1989; Ornitz et al., 1993; Osterling & Dawson, 1994; Rapin, 1991). These difficulties also have been reported by individuals with autism themselves (Cesaroni & Garber, 1991; Grandin, 1992; Williams, 1995). Incidence of sensory processing disorders (e.g., hypo- or hyperresponding to incoming sensory input, paradoxical [i.e., seemingly opposite responses to the same sensory input] responding to sensory stimuli, unusual sensory interests) reported in the autism literature ranges from 42% to 88% by some authors (Baranek, 2002; Kientz & Dunn, 1997; LeCouteur et al., 1989; Volkmar, Cohen, & Paul, 1986; Watling et al., 2001) to 30% to 100% by others (Dawson & Watling, 2000; Tomchek & Dunn, 2007).

Auditory

Differences in *auditory processing* are one of the more commonly reported sensory processing impairments, with the full range of atypical responses noted. In one retrospective chart review of developmental patterns in 200 cases with autism, Greenspan and Wieder (1997) reported that 100% of the subjects demonstrated difficulties with auditory responding. Several authors have reported auditory hypersensitivity (Bettison, 1996; Dahlgren & Gillberg, 1989; Gillberg & Coleman, 1996; Grandin & Scariano, 1986; Rimland & Edelson, 1995; Vicker, 1993). In one survey of 233 parents of children with autism (Vicker, 1993), 134 (57.5%) of the parents reported that their children were sensitive to sound, with many sensitivities to everyday environmental noises. Further, Dahlgren and Gillberg (1989) found that sensitivity to auditory stimuli in infancy was a powerful discriminator between children with and without autism. Other studies have reported auditory underresponsivity (Baranek, 1999; Osterling & Dawson, 1994; Wing, 1966), with diminished response to name frequently noted. This hyperactivity has been an early diagnostic consideration, in that children who appeared to be deaf early in life have subsequently been diagnosed with autism (Wing, 1966).

Visual

Paradoxical *visual responding* also is reported in the literature. Avoidance of eye contact and inefficient use of eye gaze have been described as early features of autism (Baranek, 1999; Gillberg & Coleman, 2000; Gillberg et al., 1990; Kientz & Dunn, 1997). These difficulties are often classified as social abnormalities; however, several authors (Dawson & Lew, 1989; Gillberg & Coleman, 2000; Gillberg et al., 1990; Miller, 1996; Wing, 1980) have explained diminished eye contact as a self-regulatory mechanism that compensates for difficulties with modulating visual input. Other studies have reported children with autism to have unusual visual inspection of objects (i.e., moving objects; LeCouteur et al., 1989; Lord et al., 1994).

Tactile

Overresponsivity to *tactile* input has also been reported in the literature (Baranek, Foster, & Berkson, 1997; Cesaroni & Garber, 1991; Grandin, 1995). In firsthand accounts, touch has been described as not necessarily painful but rather as an intense feeling that can be overwhelming and confusing (Cesaroni & Garber, 1991). Grandin (1995) noted that certain clothing textures made her extremely anxious, distracted, and fidgety. Children with higher levels of tactile hypersensitivity in one study also were more likely to display inflexible behaviors, repetitive verbalizations, visual stereotypies, and abnormally focused attention (Baranek et al., 1997). These same behaviors often are associated with early diagnostic symptoms of autism.

Attention and arousal impairments have been reported (Dawson & Lew, 1989; Ornitz, Guthrie, & Farley, 1977, 1978; Rapin, 1991; Volkmar et al., 1986) and could be explained as relating to impairments in modulating sensory input. Early studies by Ornitz and colleagues (1977, 1978) described a pattern of "disturbances in sensory modulation and motility" affecting all sensory systems in over 70% of the children with autism ages 6 years or younger in their samples. These findings were replicated in another sample (Volkmar et al., 1986), with clusters of unusual sensory and motor behaviors including no response to sound (81%), increased sensitivity to loud noises (53%), visual inspection of hands or fingers (62%), and arm flapping (52%).

Discriminative Function of Sensory Processing

Empirical data from clinical evaluations (Adrien et al., 1987; Gillberg et al., 1990), parent report measures (Dahlgren & Gillberg, 1989; Ermer & Dunn, 1998; Gillberg et al., 1990; Hoshino et al., 1982; Kientz & Dunn, 1997; Watling et al., 2001), and retrospective video analysis (Adrien et al., 1992, 1993; Baranek, 1999) are emerging to suggest that behavioral features of children with autism attributed to sensory processing differ qualitatively from children with other developmental disorders and typically developing children. These qualitative differences in sensory processing frequently have been key features in discriminating between children with autism and children with other disabilities and/or typical development.

Some data suggest that early sensory processing disorders may be among the first signs of autism (Dahlgren & Gillberg, 1989; Gillberg et al., 1990; Hoshino et al., 1982). In an early study (Hoshino et al., 1982), infants with autism did not respond to certain sounds, displayed hypersensitivity to the tastes of certain foods, and were insensitive to pain more frequently than infants developing typically or infants with other developmental disorders. More recently, sensory processing differences (e.g., overexcited when tickled, difficulties imitating movements, does not listen when spoken to, exceptionally interested in looking at things that move, unusual eye gaze to objects, plays with only hard objects) reported retrospectively by parents discriminated between children with ASDs and children ages 3 years or younger developing typically (Dahlgren & Gillberg, 1989; Gillberg et al., 1990). Further, hand and finger mannerisms, whole-body mannerisms, and unusual sensory interests (especially visual inspection of objects), as recorded on the Autism Diagnostic Interview, discriminated children with autism from those with other developmental delays (LeCouteur et al., 1989; Lord et al., 1994).

Adrien and colleagues (1987) utilized observations and frequency counts of behaviors during a structured play session to differentiate between children without disabilities, children with mental retardation, and children with autism and very low developmental ages. Although many behaviors overlapped between the groups, nine behaviors (rubbing surface, finger flicking, body rocking, repetitive jumping, decreased eye contact, limited or inappropriate social smile and laugh, using objects ritualistically, ignoring objects, and absent response to stimuli) discriminated children with autism from both children without disabilities and children with mental retardation. These findings were replicated by Rapin (1996), who found that atypical sensory modulation and motor stereotypies discriminated children with autism from children with other developmental disorders.

Sensory processing behaviors of children ages 3 to 6 years with ($n = 40$) and without ($n = 40$) autism, gathered via parent report on the Sensory Profile (SP; Dunn, 1999), also have been compared (Watling et al., 2001). Sensory processing of children with autism was significantly different from the sample without autism on 8 of 10 factors (Sensory Seeking, Emotionally Reactive, Low Endurance/Tone, Oral Sensitivity, Inattention/Distractibility, Poor Registration, Fine Motor/Perceptual, and Other). Similarly, Mayes and Calhoun (1999) reported that children with autism ($n = 143$) presented with a variety of sensory processing difficulties on an autism diagnostic screener. All of the children on this sample had 1 or more of the 10 symptoms on a somatosensory disturbance subscale (average of 6.2 symptoms). Most commonly reported items included a love of movement, roughhouse play, and climbing (91%); atypical feeding patterns (75%); unresponsive to verbal input (71%); and unusual sensory inspection of objects (68%).

Additional studies (Ermer & Dunn, 1998; Kientz & Dunn, 1997; Tomchek & Dunn, 2007) have utilized the SP (Dunn, 1994, 1999; Dunn & Westman, 1997). Kientz and Dunn (1997) used scores on the SP, in its test development phase, to determine if these scores discriminated between children with autism ($n = 32$) and without autism ($n = 64$) and which items best discriminated between the groups. Multivariate analysis showed that children with an ASD were reported to have higher rates of sensory processing dysfunction than the children without autism on all categories of the SP, with 84 of the 99 items (85%) differentiating the sensory processing skills of the groups. The items reflected both sensory modulation and praxis deficits in autism, as well as the social and behavior characteristics often utilized in differential diagnosis. Similarly, in Tomchek and Dunn (2007), 95% of the sample (*n* = 266) of children with an ASD demonstrated some degree of sensory processing dysfunction on the Short Sensory Profile (SSP; McIntosh et al., 1999) total score, with the greatest differences reported on the Underresponsive/Seeks Sensation, Auditory Filtering, and Tactile Sensitivity sections. The ASD group also performed significantly different (*p* < .001) on 92% (35 of 38) of the items, total score, and all sections of the SSP when compared to age-matched peers who were developing typically.

Ermer and Dunn (1998) sought to determine which of the nine factors on the SP best discriminated among children with autism or PDD (*n* = 38), children with attention deficit hyperactivity disorder (ADHD; *n* = 61), and children without disabilities (*n* = 1,075). The results yielded two discriminant functions: one that differentiated children with disabilities from those without disabilities and another that differentiated the two groups with disabilities from each other. Nearly 90% of the cases were classified correctly using these two functions. Specific to children with autism/PDD, 4 of the 9 factors best discriminated: a low incidence of behaviors reported within the Sensory Seeking factor, and a high incidence of behaviors noted within the Oral Sensitivity, Inattention/Distractibility, and Fine Motor/Perceptual factors.

A study by Rogers, Hepburn, and Wehner (2003) assessed parent report of sensory reactivity of 102 young children across four groups: autism (*n* = 26), Fragile X syndrome (*n* = 20), developmental disabilities of mixed etiology (*n* = 32), and children developing typically (*n* = 24). All groups were comparable in socioeconomic status, ethnic status, and overall mental age. Clinical groups were also comparable in mean chronologic ages. Parent report on the SSP (McIntosh et al., 1999) was used as the standard measure of sensory processing. Findings indicated that both children with Fragile X syndrome and children with autism had significantly more sensory responses overall than the two comparison groups, although the children with autism did not differ significantly from children with Fragile X syndrome. Correlation analysis did not establish a relationship between developmental level or IQ and sensory reactivity in the children with autism or developmental disorders groups. However, abnormal sensory reactivity had a significant relationship with overall adaptive behavior.

Investigations also have utilized retrospective video analysis to explore early sensory and motor features of children later diagnosed with autism (Adrien et al., 1992, 1993; Baranek, 1999; Osterling & Dawson, 1994; Werner, Dawson, Osterling, & Dinno, 2000). Stereotypic behaviors, auditory under- and overresponsiveness, unusual postures, and unstable visual attention were characteristic of infants later diagnosed with autism when compared to those with other developmental disorders or to children who developed typically (Adrien et al., 1992, 1993).

Baranek (1999) utilized retrospective videotape analysis to explore the predictive capability of sensorimotor observations of the sensory and social behavior of children ages 9 to 12 months who were later diagnosed with autism. She found that sensorimotor features such as social touch aversion, excessive mouthing of objects, and delayed response to name and decreased affect rating were subtle yet salient predictors of a subsequent autism diagnosis. These items also discriminated among children with autism (*n* = 11), children with developmental disabilities (*n* = 10), and children developing typically (*n* = 11). In contrast, other researchers also using retrospective videotape analysis have not found early sensorimotor abnormalities in children with ASDs (Osterling & Dawson, 1994; Werner et al., 2000).

■ ■ ■

Appendix B. Example Reinforcer Assessment

REINFORCER ASSESSMENT

Name: _____   Date: _____

INSTRUCTIONS TO CAREGIVERS: This checklist will be used to help us determine the types of events, activities, and objects your child likes so we can include them in his/her ongoing intervention. Please use a check mark (☺) to indicate the items preferred.

SOCIAL AND SENSORY REINFORCERS

- ☐ Adult attention
- ☐ Attention from specific adults

List preferred adults: _____
- ☐ Being left alone
- ☐ Time spent with peer

List preferred peers: _____
- ☐ Freedom from interference from adults
- ☐ Freedom from interference from peers

☐ A positive note to give to person of choice		☐ "Stim" time
☐ Hugs	☐ Praise	☐ Eye contact
☐ Private praise	☐ Public recognition	☐ Public praise
☐ Being rocked	☐ Being held	☐ Applause
☐ OK sign	☐ Back rub	☐ Tickles
☐ Sitting in adult's lap	☐ "Thumbs-up" sign	☐ Shaking hands
☐ "High-five" sign	☐ Pats	☐ Twirling around
☐ Swinging	☐ Being brushed	☐ Jumping
☐ Vibrator	☐ Lotion	☐ Powder
☐ Rolling up in blanket	☐ Smiles	☐ Motor play
☐ Blowing bubbles	☐ Shoes off	☐ Cologne/perfume

- ☐ List other _____
- ☐ List other _____
- ☐ List other _____
- ☐ List other _____
- ☐ List other _____
- ☐ List other _____

REINFORCER ASSESSMENT *(cont.)*

Name: _____   Date: _____

INSTRUCTIONS: Use a check mark (☺) to indicate the items preferred.

ACTIVITY REINFORCERS

☐ Music

List preferred music: _____

☐ Playing with toys

List preferred toys: _____

☐ Puzzles	☐ Computer	☐ Water play
☐ Playing outside	☐ Snack time	☐ Free time
☐ Playing with pets	☐ Riding toys	☐ Books, stories
☐ Going for a walk	☐ Making choices	☐ Helping adult
☐ Drawing	☐ Painting	☐ Being read to
☐ Job responsibilities	☐ Wearing cosmetics	☐ Visiting
☐ Wearing jewelry	☐ Special seat	☐ Balloons
☐ More independence	☐ Riding bikes	☐ Cooking

☐ List preferred materials _____

_____

☐ Computer

List preferred programs: _____

☐ Social activities

List preferred types: _____

☐ Leisure activities

List preferred types: _____

REINFORCER ASSESSMENT *(cont.)*

Name: _____   Date: _____

INSTRUCTIONS: Use a check mark (☺) to indicate the items preferred.

TANGIBLE ITEMS

☐ Chips
List preferred types _____
_____

☐ Cookies
List preferred types _____
_____

☐ Candy
List preferred types _____
_____

☐ Fruit
List preferred types _____
_____

☐ Cereal
List preferred types _____
_____

☐ Snacks
List preferred types _____
_____

☐ Drinks
List preferred types _____
_____

☐ Other preferred foods _____
_____

☐ Stickers
List preferred types _____
_____

☐ Toys
List preferred types _____
_____

☐ Games
List preferred types _____
_____

☐ List other _____

REINFORCER ASSESSMENT *(cont.)*

Name: _____   Date: _____

INSTRUCTIONS: Use a check mark (☺) to indicate the items preferred.

AREAS OF INTEREST

☐ Animals
   List preferred types: _____

☐ Weather	☐ Trucks	☐ Trains
☐ Dinosaurs	☐ Cars	☐ Science
☐ Math	☐ Numbers	☐ Shapes
☐ Machines	☐ Tools	☐ Clothes
☐ Outdoors	☐ Sports	☐ Computers

☐ List favorite TV programs _____
☐ List favorite celebrities _____
☐ List favorite colors _____
☐ List favorite movies _____
☐ List favorite songs _____
☐ List favorite places to go _____

☐ Other _____

☐ Other _____

☐ Other _____

MISCELLANEOUS INFORMATION

☐ List foods disliked: _____
☐ List noises disliked: _____
☐ List activities disliked: _____
☐ List places does not like to go: _____
_____

☐ List materials disliked: _____
☐ List animals disliked: _____
☐ List any other dislikes: _____
_____

☐ List any known fears: _____
_____

Appendix C. Evidence-Based Literature Review Methodology

Evidence-Based Practice

One of the greatest challenges facing health care systems, service providers, public education, and policymakers is to ensure that scarce resources are used efficiently. The growing interest in outcomes research and evidenced-based health care over the past 30 years, and the more recent interest in evidence-based education, can in part be explained by these system-level challenges in the United States and internationally.

In response to demands of the cost-oriented health care system in which occupational therapy practice is often embedded, occupational therapists and occupational therapy assistants routinely are asked to justify the value of the services they provide on the basis of the scientific evidence. The scientific literature provides an important source of legitimacy and authority for demonstrating the value of health care and education services. Thus, occupational therapists, other health care practitioners, and educators increasingly are called on to use the literature to inform their practices and to demonstrate the value of the interventions and instruction they provide to clients and students.

What Is an Evidence-Based Practice Perspective?

According to Law and Baum (1998), *evidence-based occupational therapy practice* "uses research evidence together with clinical knowledge and reasoning to make decisions about interventions that are effective for a specific client" (p. 131). An *evidence-based perspective* is based on the assumption that scientific evidence of the effectiveness of occupational therapy intervention can be judged to be more or less strong and valid according to a hierarchy of research designs and an assessment of the quality of the research.

AOTA uses standards of evidence modeled from standards developed in evidence-based medicine. This model standardizes and ranks the value of scientific evidence for biomedical practice using the grading system in Table 9. In this system, the highest levels of evidence include those studies that are systematic reviews of the literature, meta-analyses, and randomized controlled trials. In randomized controlled trials, the outcomes of an intervention are compared to the outcomes of a control group, and participation in either group is determined randomly. The evidence-based literature review presented here includes Level I randomized controlled trials; Level II studies, in which assignment to a treatment or a control group is not randomized (cohort study); and Level III studies, which do not have a control group. For the purposes of this review, only Level III and above studies are included.

This evidence-based literature review was initiated and supported by the AOTA as part of the Evidence-Based Literature Review project. The goal of the project is to promote evidence-based practice through a variety of dissemination efforts, including publication of the results of systematic reviews in peer-reviewed journals. A focused review question was developed by the review author in conjunction with AOTA staff

Table 9. Levels of Evidence for Occupational Therapy Outcomes Research

Levels of Evidence	Definitions
Level I	Systematic reviews, meta-analyses, randomized controlled trials
Level II	Two groups, nonrandomized studies (e.g., cohort, case control)
Level III	One group, nonrandomized (e.g., before and after, pretest and posttest)
Level IV	Descriptive studies that include analysis of outcomes (e.g., single-subject design, case series)
Level V	Case reports and expert opinion that include narrative literature reviews and consensus statements

Source. Adapted from Sackett, D. L., Rosenberg, W. M., Muir Gray, J. A., Haynes, R. B., & Richardson, W. S. (1996). Evidence-based medicine: What it is and what it isn't. *British Medical Journal, 312,* 71–72.

and project consultant and reviewed by an advisory group of content experts in ASDs. According to the consensus of the group, for the purposes of the review, the definition of *autism spectrum disorder* included autism, Asperger's syndrome, and PDD and excluded Rett syndrome and childhood disintegrative disorder. Search strategies included occupation and engagement in addition to performance-based interventions. The role of family, family coping, behavior, self-regulation, and the contextual components of intervention were also included in the search. In addition, there was consensus that multicomponent programs (e.g., DIR/floortime), as well as those programs that are adjunctive to educational or broader behavioral interventions, should be included in the review.

The review author, in conjunction with the AOTA consultant and a medical librarian with experience in evidence-based reviews, was responsible for searching the literature, selecting research studies of relevance to occupational therapy, analyzing the studies, and summarizing the information with emphasis on implications for occupational therapy practitioners.

Research Question

The following focused question guided the selection of research studies for the review and interpretation of our findings:

What is the evidence for the effect of interventions used in occupational therapy to create, establish, modify, and maintain performance and prevent disability in the areas of self-care, education/tran-sition, play/leisure, and social participation for children and adolescents with autism spectrum disorders?

Procedures

A broad search was undertaken to identify research studies for the review. Databases and sites searched included Medline, CINAHL, ERIC, PsychInfo, Social Sciences Abstracts, Sociological Abstract, Linguistics and Language Behavior Abstracts, OT Seeker, PEDro, TRIP, RehabData, Latin American and Caribbean Health Sciences Literature, and EBSCOHost. In addition, consolidated information sources, such as the Cochrane Database of Systematic Reviews and the Campbell Collaboration, also were included in the search. These databases are peer-reviewed summaries of journal articles and provide a system for clinicians and scientists to conduct evidence-based reviews of selected clinical questions and topics.

Search terms were developed by the review author and AOTA staff and reviewed by the advisory group. Terms used in the search are listed in Table 10. In addition, a filter based on one developed by McMaster University (http://www.urmc.rochester.edu/hslt/miner/digital_library/evidence_based_resources.cfm) was used to narrow the search to research studies. The review author and AOTA staff reviewed the articles according to their quality (i.e., scientific rigor, lack of bias) and levels of evidence. Guidelines for reviewing quantitative studies were based on those developed by Law and colleagues (1994, 2005) to ensure that the

Table 10. Evidence-Based Literature Review Search Terms

Category	Key Search Terms
Sample/client population	autism (excluding Rett syndrome and childhood disintegrative disorder), autism spectrum disorder, Asperger syndrome, pervasive developmental disorder
Intervention	occupational therapy, sensory integration, touch pressure, massage, therapeutic listening, auditory integration training, play, activities of daily living, social participation, assistive technology, augmentative communication, neuromotor, peer-mediated, Social Stories, perceptual motor learning, behavior intervention, applied behavioral analysis, discrete trial training, comprehensive, developmental, Treatment and Education of Autistic and Communication Handicapped Children (TEACCH), relationship-based interventions, friendship, job training, peer group, peer interaction, self-care, instrumental activities of daily living, antisocial behavior, adaptive behavior, cooperative behaviors, social skills training, family coping, coping skills, social competence, problem solving, decision-making skills, token economy, activity groups
Outcomes	self-care, education, transition to work and community, play, leisure, social participation, communication, affect, behavior

evidence is ranked according to uniform definitions of research design elements.

Articles were included in the review if they provided evidence for an intervention approach used with children or adolescents with ASDs, had been peer reviewed, were published after 1986, and addressed an intervention approach within the domain of occupational therapy. Only studies determined to be Level I, Level II, and Level III studies were included. Research studies were excluded if they were judged to be outside the domain of occupational therapy, were published before 1986, were Level IV or V evidence, used qualitative methods to the exclusion of quantitative methods, or were not published in the peer-reviewed literature. A total of 17,440 citations were reviewed, and 217 articles were reviewed to determine if they fit the criteria. Final selection of the articles was made by the review author, the AOTA consultant, and AOTA staff.

The studies included in the review (N = 49) were analyzed by the review author using structured categories and included study level, study design, number of participants, types of interventions and outcome measures, summary of results, study limitations, and implications of the study for occupational therapy. An evidence table (Appendix D) that included interpretation of findings for occupational therapy practitioners was developed and reviewed by AOTA staff and the project consultant. Among the 49 studies, 18 were Level I, 17 were Level II, and 14 were Level III. This systematic review presents an expanded synthesis of the findings under the categories that describe the studies found and the focused research question. The findings from the review were organized by the autism intervention approaches represented in the literature. The studies were categorized into the following topics: (1) sensory integration and sensory-based interventions, (2) relationship-based interventions, (3) school-based programs, (4) social skills interventions, and (5) comprehensive behavioral interventions. These categories included those interventions most likely to be used directly by occupational therapy practitioners or as part of their supportive team roles. Across the studies, certain themes consistently emerged, suggesting their importance to clinical practice.

■ ■ ■

Appendix D.
Evidence Tables

Evidence-Based Tables

SENSORY INTEGRATION; SENSORIMOTOR; SENSORY-BASED INTERVENTIONS

Author/ Year	Study Objectives	Level/Design/ Subjects	Intervention and Outcome Measures	Results	Study Limitations	Implications for Occupational Therapy
Baranek (2002)	Summarize the literature on sensory and motor development in children with autism, review sensory motor interventions for children with autism, and describe the implications	Level I—Systematic review *Subjects:* Children with autism; 29 studies of sensory motor interventions were reviewed	*Interventions:* Included sensory integration classical, sensory-integration based, sensory stimulation (e.g., touch pressure or vestibular), auditory integration training, visual and motor exercise *Measures:* Scales of behavior, interaction, play, language, IQ, autism symptoms, affect, hearing acuity, self-stimulation, and others	Several studies of sensory integration (classical and sensory-integration based), sensory stimulation, auditory integration training, visual therapy, and physical exercise demonstrated positive, but modest outcomes. Studies of AIT tended to have higher level designs, but support for AIT is minimal. Sensory integration studies tend to have weak research designs and demonstrate low effect sizes.	Most of the studies reviewed were Level III and IV. Sample sizes were often small. This review concluded that additional research is needed on sensory motor interventions.	This review has major implications for occupational therapists because sensory motor interventions often are implemented by occupational therapists. It provides a summary of intervention effects across the primary types of sensory and motor interventions and situates these interventions in the educational context. This review provides weak positive evidence for the efficacy of sensory integration for children with autism and suggests that clinical trials of sensory integration are needed.

Baranek, G. T. (2002). Effectiveness of sensory and motor interventions in autism. *Journal of Autism and Developmental Disorders, 32,* 397–422.

Bettison (1996)	Examine the effects of auditory integration training on hypersensitivity when compared to a control procedure	Level I—Randomized control trial *Subjects:* Children with autistic disorder, significant autistic symptoms, or Asperger syndrome; *N* = 80; 66 males, 14 females; age range: 3.9–17.1 years. 40 with each condition.	*Intervention:* Auditory training with the Berard approach was used. The comparison group received the same unmodified music under the same conditions. Each child attended 2 half-hour listening sessions at least 4 hours apart for 10 consecutive days.	The ABC scores improved for both groups at 1, 3, 6, and 12 months. The DBC also improved for both groups. Audiogram scores improved for both groups. None of the measures were significantly different for the auditory training group. Parent interviews indicated that the	This study was well designed and provides strong evidence. The sample size is large. The results do not support specific benefits from AIT, but support a structured listening problem.	Occupational therapists may use therapeutic listening programs in their interventions. This study suggests that potential benefits include decreased problem behaviors, improved attention, and decreased hearing sensitivity.

| | Measures: Autism Behavior Checklist (ABC), the Developmental Behavior Checklist (DBC), the Leiter International Performance Scale, Edelson's Sensory Problems Checklist, and Rimland's Hearing Sensitivity Questionnaire | children did not appear distressed with certain sounds and attention appeared to improve. It appears that both auditory integration training (AIT) and structured listening lead to reductions in hypersensitivity to sound. | |

Bettison, S. (1996). The long-term effects of audiotry training on children with autism. *Journal of Autism and Developmental Disorders, 26*, 361–375.

| Edelson, Arin, et al. (1999) | Investigate the effects of auditory integration training (AIT) over a 3-month period | Level I—Randomized clinical trial, double-blind placebo design

Subjects: Diagnosed with autism and cognitive impairment; *N* = 19; 17 male, 2 female; age range 4–39 years. Subjects were matched by age and degree of behavioral problems. | *Intervention:* The AIT device used was the Audio Tone Enhancer/Trainer, which provided modulated music to participants through headphones. Participants received AIT for 2 sessions a day for 10 days.

Measures: Aberrant Behavior Checklist (ABC), Conners Rating Scales (CRS), audiological tests, Fisher's Auditory Problems Checklist (FAPC), event-related brain potential. Measures were taken after the treatment and at 1, 2, and 3 months after treatment. | The group that received AIT improved significantly on the ABC at 1 month, then again at the 3 month follow-up. No behavioral changes were observed on the FAPC and CRS. Questionnaires to parents indicated reduced sound sensitivity, improved hearing and comprehension, and increased eye contact. | Well-designed study. The measures selected were not entirely appropriate, as 5 of 19 participants could not respond in the audiometric assessment and most were unable to complete the intelligence test. The results are inconclusive, in that it is not clear which individuals with autism are most likely to benefit from AIT. | Clients with autism who exhibit behavioral problems may benefit from AIT. Given that AIT requires special equipment, the training would become a complementary treatment to occupational therapy. Theoretically, this treatment helps to improve attention; this study demonstrated decreases in aberrant behavior. |

Edelson, S. M., Arin, D., Bauman, M., Lucas, S. E., Rudy, J. H., Sholar, M., et al. (1999). Auditory integration training: A double-blind study of behavioral and electrophysiological effects in people with autism. *Focus on Autism and Other Developmental Disabilities, 14*, 73–81.

(continued)

Evidence-Based Tables (cont.)

Author/ Year	Study Objectives	Level/Design/ Subjects	Intervention and Outcome Measures	Results	Study Limitations	Implications for Occupational Therapy
Escalona et al. (2001)	Investigate the effects of massage therapy on children with autism	Level I—Randomized controlled trial *Subjects:* Children with autism; *N* = 20; 12 boys, 8 girls; mean age 5.2 years, range 3–6 years	*Intervention:* Parents provided massage for 15 minutes prior to bedtime every night for 1 month. The parents of control group read a Dr. Seuss story for 15 minutes prior to bedtime every night for 1 month. *Measures:* Conners Teacher and Parent Scales, classroom and playground behaviors observations, sleep diaries	The children who received massage showed significant improvement on the Conners Scales' attention deficit hyperactivity disorder, restless-impulsive behavior, and emotional indexes. Stereotypical behavior decreased and social relatedness increased on the playground. On-task behavior in the classroom increased. The researchers attributed these changes to improved sleep.	This study used a small sample. The intervention was implemented for 1 month and was implemented by parents. Some of the measures were qualitative (e.g., sleep diaries).	Massage prior to bedtime decreased hyperactive, impulsive, and stereotypic behaviors. Massage is similar to some of the touch techniques used by occupational therapists. Benefits of therapeutic touch and massage may include improved sleep.

Escalona, A., Field, T., Singer-Strunck, R., Cullen, C., & Hartshorn, K. (2001). Brief Report: Improvements in the behavior of children with autism following massage therapy. *Journal of Autism and Developmental Disorders, 31,* 513–516.

Author/ Year	Study Objectives	Level/Design/ Subjects	Intervention and Outcome Measures	Results	Study Limitations	Implications for Occupational Therapy
Field et al. (1997)	Investigate the effects of touch therapy on inattentiveness (off-task behavior), touch aversion, and withdrawal.	Level I—Randomized control trial. *Subjects:* Children with autism. *N* = 22; 12 boys, 10 girls; mean age 4.5 years	*Intervention:* 11 children received touch therapy, a standard massage routine for 15 minutes per day, 2 days per week, for 4 weeks. The control group received a game (selecting different toys) and was helped for 15 minutes per day. *Measures:* Classroom observation for touch aversion, off-task behavior, orienting to irrelevant sounds, stereotypic behavior, the Autism Behavior Checklist (ABC), Early Social Communication Scales (ESCS)	In the children who received massage, touch aversion, off-task behavior, orienting to irrelevant sounds and stereotypic behavior decreased. Certain ABC subscales significantly decreased in the children who received massage. Joint attention, behavior regulation, social behavior, and initiating behavior improved significantly in the group who received massage.	Although this was defined as a randomized control trial (RCT), pre- and post-measures were compared rather than groups. Therefore, an RCT design was not used in reporting the results. Some of the measures lack standardization.	Problems with the design limit the implications for occupational therapists. Improvements in behavior related to touch therapy give some support to use of touch techniques.

Field, T., Lasko, D., Mundy, P., Henteleff, T., Kabat, S., Talpins, S., et al. (1997). Brief Report: Autistic children's attentiveness and responsivity improve after touch therapy. *Journal of Autism and Developmental Disorders, 27,* 333–338.

Study	Purpose	Design/Subjects	Intervention/Measures	Results	Conclusions
Hartishorn et al. (2001)	Examine the effects of movement therapy on children with autism	Level II—Clinical trial, nonrandomized; control group was matched on age and developmental level *Subjects:* Children with autism; *N* = 76; two groups of 38; mean age 5 years, range 3–7 years	*Intervention:* Movement therapy provided by trained movement therapists. Two sessions a week were provided for 2 months. Each session consisted of warmup, activities involving movement using hoops, obstacle courses, moving to a tambourine, and cool down. *Measures:* Children were videotaped and behaviors were rated during 18-minute sessions. Behaviors were recorded in 10-second time sample units.	At the end of 2 months, the movement therapy group spent less time wandering, less time negatively responding, less time resisting, and more time on task.	This study had many limitations. The conceptual basis for the movement therapy was not well explained; the intervention was not well described. The measure was weak, in that the pre–post measure was an 18-minute time sample. Inter-rater reliability was mediocre. The expected outcome was improved attention; however, this variable improved minimally.	This study provided weak support of movement therapy for improving on-task behavior in children with autism. Design limitations suggest that caution is needed in interpreting the results.

Hartishorn, K., Olds, L., Field, T., Delage, J., Cullen, C., & Escalona, A. (2001). Creative movement therapy benefits children with autism. *Early Child Development and Care, 186,* 1–8

Study	Purpose	Design/Subjects	Intervention/Measures	Results	Conclusions
Mudford et al. (2000)	Replicate and extend studies of auditory integration training by obtaining ratings of behaviors from teachers and parents and by including direct observational measurement of behaviors	Level I—Crossover design with random allocation *Subjects:* Children with autism; *N* = 21; 17 boys, 4 girls; mean age 9.42 years	*Intervention:* Auditory integration training. Children received 10 hours of auditory integration training across 10 days. The control group wore headphones that were nonfunctional. *Measures:* Behavior rating scales; the Aberrant Behavior Checklist; observational recordings of stereotypy, object obsessive behaviors, and disruptive behaviors; Vineland Adaptive Behavior Scale; Reynell Language Developmental Scales; Leiter.	The children who had auditory integration training did not perform better on any of the measures, including aberrant behavior, IQ, or adaptive behaviors. Their results completely contradict Rimland and Edelson (1995). Parents reported improvement in behavior; however, the objective, observational data did not confirm their reports.	Some of the children responded in a positive way to the AIT; however, these results were masked by the overall group data. This study used many measures and had a strong designs, therefore, the limitations are few.	This study is relevant to occupational therapists and does not support the use of AIT. Results appear valid and should not be ignored when making clinical decisions about the use of AIT.

Mudford, O. C., Cross, B. A., Breen, S., Cullen, C., Reeves, D., Gould, J., et al. (2000). Auditory integration training for children with autism: No behavioral benefits detected. *American Journal on Mental Retardation, 105,* 118–129.

(continued)

Evidence-Based Tables (cont.)

Author/ Year	Study Objectives	Level/Design/ Subjects	Intervention and Outcome Measures	Results	Study Limitations	Implications for Occupational Therapy
Sinha et al. (2005)	Determine the effectiveness of AIT and other methods of sound therapy in individuals with ASDs	Level I—Systematic review (Cochrane reviews) *Subjects:* Persons with autism spectrum disorders, including pervasive developmental disorders	*Interventions:* Auditory integration training using Berard's method, Tomatis method, or Samonas Sound Therapy *Measures:* Measures of cognitive ability, autism symptoms, hyperacusis, auditory processing, behavioral problems, attention, activity level, quality of life, and adverse events	Six trials were included. The largest studies did not report a difference when using AIT. One small crossover trial reported no long-term benefits. Three small trials reported an improvement in the Aberrant Behavior Checklist. Further research is required to determine the effectiveness of sound therapies.	This review was well done and represents the highest level of evidence.	This review is important to occupational therapists in that it provides a bottom line on the effectiveness of auditory integration training. Unfortunately, the bottom line states that there is not conclusive evidence of effectiveness and that additional research is needed.

Sinha, Y., Silove, N., Wheeler, D., & Williams, K. (2005). Auditory integration training and other sound therapies for autism spectrum disorders. *Cochrane Database of Systematic Reviews*, Issue 1. Art No.: CD003681. DOI: 10.100 2/14651858. CD003681.pub2.

| Zollweg et al. (1997) | Evaluate the efficacy of auditory integration training (AIT) on children with multiple disabilities | Level I—Randomized controlled trial

Subjects: Children and adults with cognitive impairment or autism. $N = 30$; 8 females, 22 males; age from 7 to 24 years. 15 in the treatment group and 15 in the control group. | *Intervention:* AIT using Audio Enhancer Trainer. The music was filtered and modulated, and volume was controlled. Each subject received 20 half-hour sessions. The control group appeared to have received no treatment.

Measures: Audiological assessments of hearing sensitivity, Aberrant Behavior Checklist | The two groups did not differ in hearing sensitivity. Both groups made similar improvements in behavior. AIT did not result in any significant changes in hearing or behavior. | The study was well designed, although use of different diagnoses could confound the findings. The control group had more persons with cognitive impairment; the treatment group had more persons with autism. | This Level I study did not support AIT. The results should be considered when making recommendations to families regarding potential effects of AIT. |

Zollweg, W., Palm, D., & Vance, V. (1997). The efficacy of auditory integration training: A double blind study. *American Journal of Audiology, 6*(3), 39–47.

Dawson & Galpert (1990)	Explore if imitative play used daily by mothers for 2 weeks increases social engagement and creative toy play	Level III—Pre- and posttest with one group *Subjects:* Children with autism below age 7; 15 children began the study, 14 completed it	*Intervention:* Given two sets of toys, mothers were instructed to imitate their child using an identical toy. Mothers were instructed to perform the imitation 20 minutes each day. *Measures:* Children were videotaped during free play and were scored using the levels of the Uzgiris-Hunt Scale of Gestural Imitation. Children were scored with familiar and novel toys.	Children demonstrated more facial gaze at mother's face. They demonstrated less gaze at mother's actions with toys. The majority of children showed increases in the number of toy changes and different schemes.	This study has significant limitations. A small, nonrandomized sample was used with no control group, the measures were subjective, and the intervention was minimal (2 weeks).	Given a weak design, this study has minimal implications for occupational therapy practitioners. It does support a child-centered approach in which the child's actions are imitated in order to encourage more complex play.

Dawson, G., & Galpert, L. (1990). Mothers' use of initiative play for facilitating social responsiveness and toy play in young autistic children. *Development and Psychopathology, 2,* 151–162.

| Field et al. (2001) | Examine the effectiveness of adults imitating the behaviors of children with autism on the children's social behaviors | Level I—Randomized trial

Subjects: Children with autism; *N* = 20; 10 girls, 10 boys; all nonverbal; age range 4–6 years, mean 5.4 | *Intervention:* The treatment was 3 sessions. One group received imitation (experimental), the other group only provided contingent responses, that is, participated in natural play interactions (control).

Measures: Each session was videotaped and frequency of social behaviors was coded. Both negative and positive social and play behaviors were coded. | At the time of the second session, the group that was imitated demonstrated less time being inactive and playing alone, and more time showing objects, showing distal social behaviors (looking at, vocalizing to, and smiling at the adult), imitating, and engaging in reciprocal play. During the third session, the imitated group showed more mirror play and more social behaviors. | The treatment in this study was very brief (3 sessions). The sample size was small (10 in each group). The measures appeared subjective and were not standardized, although inter-rater reliability was high. Follow-up measures were not completed. | Occupational therapists have opportunities to imitate the child during one-on-one intervention sessions. Use of imitation during play activities may increase the child's social interest and behaviors. Imitation of the child's behavior appears to encourage reciprocal play. The study's findings are intriguing but must be viewed as a pilot study. |

Field, T., Field, T., Sanders, C., & Nadel. J. (2001). Children with autism display more social behaviors after repeated imitation sessions. *Autism, 5,* 317–323.

(continued)

Evidence-Based Tables (cont.)

Author/ Year	Study Objectives	Level/Design/ Subjects	Intervention and Outcome Measures	Results	Study Limitations	Implications for Occupational Therapy
Greenspan & Wieder (1997)	Examine symptoms, processing difficulties, early development, and response to treatment of a large cohort of children with autism spectrum disorders	Level III—Descriptive chart review that included pre- and posttests for a group of children treated in a single practice. No inferential statistical analyses. *Subjects:* Children diagnosed with autism (75%) or pervasive developmental disorder not otherwise specified (25%); *N* = 200; age range 22 months–4 years at the time of initial evaluation. In a substudy, 20 of the optimal outcome group between 5 and 10 years were compared to a matched control sample of children without disabilities.	*Intervention:* Relationship-based individual difference, interactive intervention model was used (floortime). In addition, each child received comprehensive services, including speech and occupational therapy. Intervention was provided for a minimum of 2 years. *Measures:* Childhood Autism Rating Scale. Twenty "good outcome" children were compared to 14 age-matched children developing typically and 12 with continuing difficulties using the Vineland Adaptive Behavior Scales, Functional Emotional Assessment Scale (FEAS). Affective interaction, muscle tone, motor planning, and sensory processing were informally measured.	Overall outcomes were presented: 116 (58%) of the 200 had good to outstanding outcomes; 50 (25%) had medium outcomes; and 34 (17%) continued to have problems. When good outcome children were compared to age-matched children who were developing typically, they were similar on the FEAS. The good outcome group scored well on the Vineland (average or above average).	This chart review used a retrospective design to examine patterns of improvement in young children with autism spectrum disorders. Most of the children were treated for a long period of time and were involved in multiple treatments; therefore, the variables responsible for improvement cannot be identified. The goal was to identify which children may demonstrate the most improvement.	This detailed descriptive study provides an explanation of behavior in children with autism spectrum disorders; however, without statistical analysis, this study does not offer evidence for the effectiveness of the approach studied (floortime). As a descriptive study, its purpose was to identify variables for further study. Floortime can be incorporated into occupational therapy and is consistent with child-centered play and aspects of sensory integration approaches. This review presents clinical evidence rather than research evidence.

Greenspan, S. I., & Wieder, S. (1997). Developmental patterns and outcomes in infants and children with disorders in relating and communicating: A chart review of 200 cases of children with autistic spectrum diagnoses. *Journal of Developmental and Learning Disorders, 1,* 87–142.

| Hwang & Hughes (2000) | Review studies of the effectiveness of social interactive training on early social communicative skills of children with autism | Level I—Systematic review of 16 studies

Subjects: Children with autism; *N* = 64; 84% boys, 16% | *Intervention:* Social interactive strategies used were (1) contingent imitation, (2) naturally occurring reinforcement, | Time delay resulted in increases in verbal responses, greetings, and requesting skills. Environmental arrangement resulted | This review points to some limitations in the studies, such as small sample sizes, nonrandomized samples, and | This review has important implications for occupational therapy. Many of the strategies defined can be implemented |

Author/Year	Study Objective/Intervention	Level/Design/Subjects	Measures	Results	Conclusions	Comments
		girls; age range 2–12 years, mean age 6.5 years	(3) waiting for child's response, and (4) environmental arrangement *Measures:* Most studies used direct observation of eye gaze; requesting action, object, or information; greetings; joint attention; expressing affection; imitative play; naming pictures; and verbal responding	in increases in verbal requests, appropriate responses and initiations, and prolonged social interactions. Contingent imitation results increased eye gaze, positive affect, and attending. Nine of the 16 studies measured and reported generalization of skills. Six studies used a follow-up measure, 5 maintained positive findings, and 1 was inconsistent.	lack of standardized measures. They recommend that training be implemented with younger children, that strategies be combined, that time delay (i.e., waiting for child's response) appears quite effective, that findings vary across different types of children, that generalization needs more study, that studies should examine intervention implemented for longer periods of time, and that fidelity of treatment needs to be assessed.	by occupational therapists to engage children and promote social interaction. Combining these techniques may be an effective way to enhance children's engagement and social interaction skills.

Hwang, B., & Hughes, C. (2000). The effects of social interactive training on early social communicative skills of children with autism. *Journal of Autism and Developmental Disorders, 30,* 331–343.

Author/Year	Study Objective/Intervention	Level/Design/Subjects	Interventions	Results	Conclusions	Comments
Kasari et al. (2006)	Evaluate the effectiveness of a combined developmental and behavioral approach on joint attention and symbolic play skills in children with autism	Level I—Randomized controlled trial *Subjects:* Children with autism; *N* = 58; age range 3–4 years; 20 in joint attention, 21 in play, and 17 in control groups	*Interventions:* Joint attention group: Discrete trial training for 5–8 minutes to prime the 22- to 25-minute session with a natural, play-based approach (responsive and facilitative interactive methods). Symbolic play approach: Followed the child's lead, imitated the child, and adapted the activity to allow for success by the child (session of similar length as joint attention).	Both intervention groups improved significantly compared to the controls on specific behaviors. Children in the joint attention group improved in joint attention that generalized to other environments. Examples of these behaviors include giving toys, showing toys, and coordinated joint looks.	Study is of good quality and the design was strong (large sample size, multiple measures, and adequate dosage). The intervention was intensive (30 minutes daily for 5 to 6 weeks). The intervention combined both behavioral and child-driven milieu teaching, making it difficult to determine what elements produced the effects. However, this combined approach is similar to interventions provided by interdisciplinary teams.	This study examined the effects of a combined intervention designed to generalize the effects of discrete trial training by adding playful social interaction focused on specific goals. The intervention was effective in helping children with ASDs develop pretend play skills and joint attention, which are almost always delayed and often are resistant to change.

(continued)

Evidence-Based Tables (cont.)

Author/ Year	Study Objectives	Level/Design/ Subjects	Intervention and Outcome Measures	Results	Study Limitations	Implications for Occupational Therapy
Kasari et al. (2006) (cont.)			*Control group:* No additional intervention by early intervention program, but provided the same amount of 1:1 or small group contact. Intervention period was 5–6 weeks. *Measures:* Early Social Communication Scales, Structured Play Assessment, caregiver–child interaction	Children in the symbolic play group had higher levels of symbolic play with their mothers and higher mastery levels of play on the play and interaction assessments.		This study supports the child-driven, playful approaches used in occupational therapy. The findings suggest that occupational therapists can use these approaches to help children generalize the skills they learn in behavioral intervention.

Kasari, C., Freeman, S., & Paparella, T. (2006). Joint attention and symbolic play in young children with autism: A randomized controlled intervention study. *Journal of Child Psychology and Psychiatry and Allied Disciplines, 4,* 611–620.

Author/ Year	Study Objectives	Level/Design/ Subjects	Intervention and Outcome Measures	Results	Study Limitations	Implications for Occupational Therapy
Koegel et al. (1996)	Compare the effects of two different types of parent training on parents' global style of interactions during unstructured home activities	Level II—Two groups, nonrandomized study (cohort) *Subjects:* Families of children with autism; *N* = 17; preschool-age children, mean developmental age near 3 years	*Intervention:* Individual target behavior (ITB) training was compared to pivotal response training (PRT). In ITB, parents target a specific skill that they train the child to perform using behavioral techniques. In PRT, parents focus on key pivotal behaviors. New behaviors are encouraged in the context of already mastered skills. Naturally occurring reinforcers are used in PRT. *Measures:* Families were videotaped during dinner. Interaction was scored by blinded evaluators for happiness, interest, stress, and communication style.	The parents trained using PRT showed overall more positive parent–child interaction. The PRT condition produced more positive changes for happiness, interest, stress, and communication style.	Limitations include lack of randomization. The measure (videotape of dinner) may be biased toward the PRT training. The measure appears to be somewhat subjective (happiness, interest). One design strength was that the evaluators were blind to the condition and order when scoring the videotapes.	PRT is a good fit for occupational therapy. The principles (allow the child to participate in choice of activity, intersperse maintenance tasks with new acquisition tasks, reinforce child's attempts to respond, and use naturally occurring reinforcers) are generally held principles in occupational therapy interventions. The focus on pivotal behaviors potentially can improve the child's ability to attend to and learn many skills beyond those that are the immediate focus of intervention.

Koegel, R. L., Bimbela, A., & Schreibman, L. (1996). Collateral effects of parent training on family interactions. *Journal of Autism and Developmental Disorders, 26,* 347–359.

| LeGoff (2004) | Determine the effects of LEGO® social skills group on social competence | Level II—Nonrandomized trial; subjects served as own control

Subjects: Children with autistic disorder, Asperger syndrome, or PDD–NOS: $N = 47$; 34 males, 13 females; mean age 10.6 and 10.10 for two groups | *Intervention:* LEGO therapy consisted of the following elements: (1) Children played with LEGOs and followed simple social rules, (2) points were awarded for appropriate social behaviors, (3) siblings attended as helpers, (4) therapeutic aides facilitated the play, (5) group members checked in and described personal experiences, (6) free play was allowed, (7) group members made joint decisions, and (8) families developed a support network.

Measures: (1) Count of number of self-initiated social contacts, (2) duration of social interactions, and (3) Social Interaction subscale of the Gilliam Autism Rating Scale (GAS) | Significant differences were found between treatment and control phases for all three dependent variables (social initiation, duration of social interactions, and social interaction per the GAS), which all showed significant improvement following the LEGO therapy. There was a 175% increase in duration of social interaction with peers in free play. | Nonrandomized sample, limited description of LEGO therapy, lack of theoretical basis for study, which limits generalizability | Structured activity can improve social competence in children with autism when it includes: (1) behavioral supports (rewards), (2) peer support (siblings and peers used), (3) rules to guide social behavior, and (4) guided practice in social problem solving. In particular, this study demonstrates the effectiveness of specific play materials (LEGOs), a particular occupational form. It also demonstrates the effectiveness of forming a social group. All of these methods are used in occupational therapy. |

LeGoff, D. B. (2004). Use of LEGO as a therapeutic medium for improving social competence. *Journal of Autism and Developmental Disorders, 34*, 557–571.

(continued)

Author/ Year	Study Objectives	Level/Design/ Subjects	Intervention and Outcome Measures	Results	Study Limitations	Implications for Occupational Therapy
LeGoff & Sherman (2006)	Compare social competence and autistic behaviors in children who received LEGO® therapy and those who received comparable social skills interventions; examine variables that predict outcome	Level II—Retrospective pre–post control group design using a matched sample of children. Two groups nonrandomized. *Subjects: N =* 117; 60 in the LEGO group (49 males, 11 females), 57 in the control group (47 males, 10 females); children diagnosed with autistic disorder (50), Asperger syndrome (55), or PDD–NOS (12)	*Intervention:* In the LEGO intervention, children participated in a LEGO Club where they learn to collaborate to build LEGO structures. The control group received the same amount and types of individual and group therapy as the children in the LEGO therapy. *Measures:* Vineland Adaptive Behavior social domain, GARS Social Interaction Scale. Secondary analysis used the Wechsler IQ, Vineland Adaptive Behavior composite, and Wechsler verbal IQ.	A significant interaction between time (pre- and posttests) and group (control and LEGO) revealed that the LEGO group improved more on the Vineland social domain and scored lower (improved) on the GARS Social Interaction Scale. Secondary analyses indicated that the child's function level at the beginning predicted social adaptive behaviors. Language function also predicted social competency outcomes. Language predicted outcomes more for the Asperger group than for the autistic disorder group.	The intervention was not well described. This retrospective study used data that had been collected in the past. The samples were nonrandomized. Also, the evaluator (first author) was not blind to group assignment.	LEGOs are a structured play activity similar to many occupational therapy activities. The intervention involves sharing and collaboration, which are frequently emphasized in occupational therapy groups. The fact that long-term outcomes were demonstrated for social competence and social interaction suggests that construction play activities in occupational therapy can achieve the same goals.

LeGoff, D. B., & Sherman, M. (2006). Long-term outcome of social skills intervention based on interactive LEGO play. *Autism, 1,* 317–329.

Author/ Year	Study Objectives	Level/Design/ Subjects	Intervention and Outcome Measures	Results	Study Limitations	Implications for Occupational Therapy
Mahoney & Perales (2005)	Compare the effects of relationship-focused early intervention on young children with PDD to those with other developmental disabilities	Level III—Nonrandomized into two groups, each of which receives the same treatment; before-and-after measures *Subjects:* Young children with either pervasive developmental disorders (PDD) or other developmental disabilities (DD); *N =* 50; children with PDD: 10 with autism, 3 with autism and	*Intervention:* This relationship-focused intervention involved teaching mothers to become more responsive to their children. It incorporated transactional intervention and the impact that it has on pivotal developmental behaviors. Treatment was provided weekly for 1 hour sessions for approximately 1 year.	Behaviors as measured by the Child Behavior Rating Scale improved; children with PDD made greater improvements than children with DD. Mothers made significant increases in responsiveness as measured by MBRS. Mothers of children with PDD increased responsiveness more than mothers with DD. Children made significant gains in	This study did not use a control group, but compared two groups who received the same intervention approach. The intervention approach was defined theoretically, but was not explicitly operationalized in the report. The yearlong intervention allowed for intervening variables to influence the results. The study's theoretic base is strong.	This study has limitations, but its conceptual base is both consistent with and useful to occupational therapists. This approach gives practical guidance to a family-centered approach by emphasizing the mother's interaction with the child. In addition, it supports the importance of social–emotional development to competence in all developmental

	Subjects	Measures / Intervention	Results	Comments
	mental retardation, 7 with PDD; children with DD: 13 with DD, 14 with speech and language delay, and 3 other; age range 12–54 months, mean 26.4 months	*Measures:* Transdisciplinary Play-Based Assessment, a child development profile; the Infant Toddler Social Emotional Assessment; and the Temperament and Atypical Behavior Scale. Pivotal developmental behavior was measured using the Child Behavior Rating Scale. Parent interaction was measured using the Maternal Behavior Rating Scale (MBRS).	development and social-emotional functioning: Rates of development changed from 20% to 259%. Children with PDD made greater improvements on the developmental measures than children with DD. Changes in mothers' responsiveness accounted for 20% of the variance in changes in children's pivotal developmental behavior. Pivotal behavior accounted for an average of 9.5% of the variance in children's change on the developmental measures.	skills. The concept of recognizing and building on a child's pivotal behaviors is useful to occupational therapists. A strong clinical trial is needed to further support this intervention.

Mahoney, G., & Perales, F. (2005). Relationship-focused early intervention with children with pervasive developmental disorders and other disabilities: A comparative study. *Developmental and Behavioral Pediatrics, 26,* 77–85.

Redefer & Goodman (1989)	Examine the effects of pet-facilitated therapy on social behavior	Level III—One group, measured through four phases: Baseline, intervention, baseline, and follow-up *Subjects:* Children with autism who attended one center; $N = 12$; 9 boys, 3 girls; age range 5–10 years	*Intervention:* The children were encouraged to handle a dog, then to pet and identify the dog's body parts. Then the children were involved in taking care of and playing with the therapy dog. *Measures:* Play was rated through a time sampling procedure. Isolation and social interaction were rated.	Social interaction increased when the dog was introduced into the play session. Repeated measures analysis of variance revealed no significant improvement in isolation and social interaction across the phases; therefore, the dog brought some improvement that eroded over time.	This study used a small sample. By alternating baseline and intervention, the subjects served as their own control. The dog did not appear to cause a substantial effect over time. It appeared that the novelty of the dog may have improved social interaction for a brief period.
					Occupational therapy practitioners sometimes use pets and dogs in their intervention. The benefits of using pets are many; however, this study suggests that they may not be maintained. Perhaps including a family pet in therapy sessions may produce more sustained effects. This study has limited relevance to occupational therapy, given a weak design and limited findings.

Redefer, L. A., & Goodman, J. F. (1989). Brief Report: Pet-facilitated therapy with autistic children. *Journal of Autism and Developmental Disorders, 19,* 461–467.

(continued)

Evidence-Based Tables (cont.)

Author/ Year	Study Objectives	Level/Design/ Subjects	Intervention and Outcome Measures	Results	Study Limitations	Implications for Occupational Therapy
Schleien et al. (1990)	Investigate the effects of four social levels of play (isolate, dyadic, group, and team) on the appropriate play behavior of children with autism	Level III—One group, nonrandomized. Baseline phase, then children did each of the four social play levels. *Subjects:* Children with autism; *N* = 17; 16 males, 1 female; age range 5–12; children in two different special education classrooms	*Intervention:* In two 30-minute sessions per week, the students rotated through 4 different levels of social play: isolate, dyadic, group, team. Peers without disabilities were trained to facilitate subjects' involvement. *Measures:* Appropriate play behaviors were measured.	The frequency of appropriate behaviors was lowest in the isolate play condition when compared to the other conditions.	The sample size was low and was a convenience sample. The intervention would be difficult to replicate, as it involved both peers without disabilities and staff, and included many different gym activities that were not well defined or controlled. The measure was subjective and the evaluators were not blinded.	This study had many threats to validity and therefore has minimal relevance to occupational therapy.

Schleien, S. J., Mustonen, T., Rynders, J. E., & Fox, A. (1990). Effects of social play activities on the play behavior of children with autism. *Journal of Leisure Research, 22,* 317–328.

Author/ Year	Study Objectives	Level/Design/ Subjects	Intervention and Outcome Measures	Results	Study Limitations	Implications for Occupational Therapy
Schleien et al. (1995)	Evaluate the effects of inclusive art activities designed to encourage cooperation and positive interactions on the frequency of social intervention between participants with and without autism	Level III—One group, nonrandomized, multiple baseline *Subjects:* Students with autism; *N* = 15 students with autism (age range 4–11 years; 2 girls, 13 boys) and 53 students without disabilities. Students with autism were divided into two groups, older and younger.	*Intervention:* Baseline comprised activities in the KIDSPACE museum with the art teacher. In intervention, the children without disabilities were instructed to interact with the children with autism. Staff was oriented to the children's training. *Measures:* Frequency of positive social interactions initiated by students with autism, and frequency of interactions directed toward students with autism by peers without disabilities, and appropriate and inappropriate behaviors.	For the older group, positive interactions directed toward the students with autism by peers increased significantly, but interactions initiated by students with autism remained low. In the younger group, interaction did not increase. Social interactions increased initially, but increases were not sustained.	Limitations include lack of randomized sampling, small sample size, and measures that appeared subjective and nonstandardized.	This study has relevance to occupational therapy because it examines a community-based activity (a community art program) that could be accessible to all children. It uses and builds on an inclusive model of education. Although some improvement in social interaction was noted, the results were minimal, suggesting that this outcome is difficult to achieve in naturalistic community settings.

Schleien, S. J., Mustonen, T., & Rynders, J. E. (1995). Participation of children with autism and nondisabled peers in a cooperatively structured community art program. *Journal of Autism and Developmental Disorders, 25,* 397–413.

Wieder & Greenspan (2005)	Report on a 10- to 15-year follow-up on 16 children with autism spectrum disorders who received comprehensive developmental, individual-difference, relationship-based (DIR) approach	Level III—Descriptive follow-up of a group who had received comprehensive DIR/floortime approach *Subjects:* Children diagnosed with pervasive developmental or autism spectrum disorders; *N* = 16; all male; age range when treatment began: 24–30 months, age range at follow-up: 12–17 years	*Intervention:* DIR/floortime approach is a developmental approach that focuses on relating, communicating, and thinking; addresses sensory processing and motor planning; and involves family interaction. *Measures:* Parent interviews, Functional Developmental Emotional Questionnaire, child interviews, school reports, Child Behavior Check List (CBCL)	Parent-rated functional emotional developmental levels were high. The CBCL competency scores were classified as: normal—82%, borderline—12%, not normal—6%. Sensory profiles were normal in 53%–93% of the categories. Academic grades were excellent to average. Qualitative findings suggested that all 16 boys had very positive outcomes, particularly related to social competence.	This study's design is quite weak, with numerous threats to validity. Without the rigors of research design in place, this report is best categorized as program evaluation. Most of the measures are weak and not comparable. The reader does not know how the sample was selected. School grades and reports would be influenced by external variables and should be interpreted with caution. The events and interventions during the follow-up period were not measured or reported.	Although developmental, individual-difference, relationship-based approaches are frequently embedded in occupational therapy interventions, this study has minimal relevance for occupational therapists given the weak design and numerous threats to validity. Although follow-up studies of long periods (e.g., 12 years) are needed, many intervening variables, inevitably not measured, threaten the association between the intervention (at 2 years) and outcome (at 12–17 years).

Wieder, S., & Greenspan, S. (2005). Can children with autism master the core deficits and become empathetic, creative, and reflective? *Journal of Developmental and Learning Disorders, 9*, 1–22.

SCHOOL-BASED PROGRAMS

Charman et al. (1997)	Examine the effects of using prompted, highly structured play tasks to increase pretend play	Level II—Two groups, nonrandomized *Subjects:* A group of children with autism (*N* = 22; 18 males, 4 females; mean age 11.7 years) was compared to a group with cognitive disability (*N* = 18; 7 males, 11 females; mean age 12.4 years)	*Intervention:* The procedure involved prompted play. Each group received 15 trials. *Measures:* Play during the trials was videotaped and developmental level of play was rated.	Both groups demonstrated object substitution (pretend play) when prompted. Children with cognitive disability produced novel pretend play. Children with autism produced situationally appropriate object substitution.	This study compared two different groups of participants, but not two interventions. The results differed based on the children's mental ages. Interpretation of the measures is somewhat subjective.	Occupational therapists use play in their interventions. This study suggests that pretend play can be prompted in children with autism, but specific prompts are not explained in detail. The report's usefulness is limited, given incomplete information about the intervention and measures.

Charman, T., Swettenham, J., & Baron-Cohen, S. (1997). Infants with autism: An investigation of empathy, pretend play, joint attention, and imitation. *Developmental Psychology, 33*, 781–789.

(continued)

Evidence-Based Tables *(cont.)*

Author/ Year	Study Objectives	Level/Design/ Subjects	Intervention and Outcome Measures	Results	Study Limitations	Implications for Occupational Therapy
Ozonoff & Cathcart (1998)	Evaluate the effectiveness of the Treatment and Education of Autistic and Communication Handicapped Children (TEACCH)-based home program on young children	Level II—Two groups, nonrandomized *Subjects:* Children with autism; *N* = 22; 11 in each group, 9 boys and 2 girls in each; age range 2–6 years	*Intervention:* The treatment group received home-based TEACCH program services. The home program was 10 weeks. Families met weekly with two therapists to plan interventions for the child based on a developmental profile. Parents then implemented the interventions. The intervention emphasized teaching using the visual sense. *Measures:* The Psychoeducational Profile–Revised (PEP–R), Childhood Autism Rating Scale (CARS)	The group receiving the TEACCH intervention demonstrated significantly more improvement than the control group on the PEP–R scores. The four scales that improved the most were imitation, fine motor, gross motor, and cognitive performance.	Limitations included lack of randomization and reliance on the parents to carry out the interventions. It lacked a follow-up measurement.	The TEACCH program has been well researched and has been adopted by many school systems. It also has evolved over time based on the studies that have been completed. Occupational therapy practitioners may work in a program that uses the TEACCH model. This study provides information regarding the types of skill changes that may result.
Panerai et al. (2002)	Compare effects of the TEACCH program with an integrated education program on intelligence and adaptive behavior in children with autism or intellectual disability	Level II—Nonrandomized groups matched by gender and diagnosis *Subjects:* Children with autism or severe intellectual disability; *N* = 16; 8 in each group; all male; mean age 9 years	*Interventions:* Children in the control group attended regular schools with support teachers. Children in the experimental group received the TEACCH program. This individualized program emphasizes environment adaptation and alternative communication. The interventions were	In the children who received TEACCH, scores on the PEP–R improved significantly time one to time two in imitation, perception, gross motor skills, hand–eye coordination, cognitive performance, total scores, and developmental ages. In the control group, only hand–eye coordina-	Sample size was small and selection was nonrandom. Although this design included two groups, the groups were not compared. Only time was compared, with improvements across time reported. This statistical analysis is faulty and puzzling given that the groups were matched.	Studies of TEACCH generally show positive results, most often with low to moderate effects. This study is similar in that TEACCH was associated with positive change; however, the study design was faulty and therefore did not provide definitive results. TEACCH techniques are used

Ozonoff, S., & Cathcart, K. (1998). Effectiveness of a home program intervention for young children with autism. *Journal of Autism and Developmental Disorders, 28*, 25–32.

by occupational therapists, particularly using environmental adaptation and visual aids for communication. These techniques appear to have some efficacy; however, the results of this study must be applied with caution given the small sample size, the foreign setting (Italy), and weak statistical analysis.

applied for 1 year. The study took place in Italy.

Measures: PsychoEducational Profile–Revised (PEP–R), Vineland Adaptive Behavior Scale (VABS)

tion improved. On the VABS, the children who received TEACCH improved in personal, daily living, leisure, and total skills. The control group improved in daily living skills only. The TEACCH and control groups were not directly compared.

Limited information is provided about the control group. Given that the control group was not used as a statistical comparison, this study is best categorized as Level III.

Panerai, S., Ferrante, L., & Zingale, M. (2002). Benefits of the Treatment and Education of Autistic and Communication Handicapped Children (TEACCH) programme as compared with a non-specific approach. *Journal of Intellectual Disability Research, 46,* 318–327.

| Rogers et al. (1986) | Describe children's developmental changes after 6 months of a preschool program that used play as a primary vehicle for developmental change | Level III—Descriptive study, using before and after measures.

Subjects: Children with autism, PDD, or severe emotional disabilities and those with cognitive delays; *N* = 26; 13 with autism according to the Childhood Autism Rating Scales (CARS; mean age 47.9 months), 10 who scored in the autistic range on the CARS (mean age 51.3 months), 3 who were not rated on the CARS

Intervention: The preschool program emphasized positive affect, nonverbal communication, communication embedded in play, promotion of social relationships, handling of unwanted behaviors consistently, and provision of classroom structure. Intervention using this model was provided for 6 months in a preschool setting.

Measures: Early Intervention Profile, Play Observation Scale, parent–child play interaction | Children's play and developmental skills improved more than was expected by initial rates. Change was significantly different than expected growth in cognition, communication, and social-emotional skills. The authors suggest that the positive results were related to attention to child's nonverbal communication, reciprocal behaviors, emphasis on positive affect, and use of play. | This study used a convenience sample from the setting that implemented this preschool program. Measures were not standardized. Lack of a control group or a baseline limits the design.

The concepts studied are consistent with occupational therapy approaches. The program focused on play and responsive adult/peer interaction, as do occupational therapy approaches. Although this preschool program is similar to occupational therapy interventions, the design has numerous threats to validity that need to be considered in applying the results. |

Rogers, S. J., Herbison, J. M., Lewis, H. C., Pantone, J., & Rels, K. (1986). An approach for enhancing the symbolic communicative and interpersonal functioning of young children with autism or severe emotional handicaps. *Journal of the Division for Early Childhood, 10(2),* 135–148.

(continued)

Evidence-Based Tables (cont.)

Author/ Year	Study Objectives	Level/Design/ Subjects	Intervention and Outcome Measures	Results	Study Limitations	Implications for Occupational Therapy
Rogers & DiLalla (1991)	Evaluate the effects of a developmental-based instruction model on preschool children with autism and preschool children with behavioral and developmental disorders	Level III—Descriptive study that involved retrospective analysis of children's change in developmental rate before and after approximately 8–12 months of intervention, 3–4 hours per day *Subjects:* Children with autism or PDD (*N* = 49; mean age 45.77 months) and children with behavioral or developmental disorders (*N* = 27; mean age 50.2 months); total N N = 76	*Intervention:* This developmental approach used positive affect, emphasis on pragmatics, positive adult and peer relationship, classroom structure and routine, and consistent handling of unwanted behaviors. *Measures:* Mental age was measured using the Merrill-Palmer or the Bayley Scales. Developmental profile was assessed using the Early Intervention Development Profile and the Childhood Autism Rating Scale (CARS). Language was measured using a variety of tools.	The children with autism improved more during the intervention period than was expected based on their initial developmental rate. The rate of developmental improvement did not differ between the groups, although the authors predicted that the autism group would make slower progress.	This study can be characterized as a program evaluation as it did not include a control group. During this time, methods, staff, and environments would change. Without a well-defined intervention, the results are difficult to generalize. In addition, a number of different measures were used over time, then combined using mental or developmental age. Age scores have greater standard error.	Elements of this intervention are similar to those used by occupational therapists. The results suggest that comprehensive developmental approaches with emphasis on positive interactions can accelerate developmental changes. When comprehensive interventions such as this one are evaluated, it is difficult to analyze what specific methods were associated with improved developmental competence.
Salt et al. (2002)	Evaluate the effectiveness of a developmentally based early intervention program on children's performance and parent stress	Level II—Nonrandomized, two-group comparison. *Subjects:* Children with childhood autism; *N* = 17; 12 in experimental group and 5 in control group (on waiting list); mean age 42.3 months	*Intervention:* The Scottish early intervention program was not described, other than it is a social developmental approach. *Measures:* Bayley Scales of Infants' Development, British Picture Vocabulary Scale, Vineland Adaptive Behavior Scales,	The treatment group demonstrated significantly more improvement than the control group on socialization, daily living skills, and motor and adaptive behavior. They also demonstrated more improvement in imitation, joint attention, and social interaction. Parent stress was	Limitations include lack of randomization and the group sizes not being equal. The sample size was small. The study lacks follow-up.	Relevance to occupational therapy is not clear, as the intervention was not described. The approach appeared to be holistic and family centered; therefore, the results may support occupational therapy interventions.

Rogers, S. J., & DiLalla, D. L. (1991). A comparative study of the effects of a developmentally based instructional model on young children with autism and young children with other disorders of behavior and development. *Topics in Early Childhood Special Education, 11(2)*, 29–47.

		Preverbal Communication Schedule, MacArthur Communication Development Inventories, Symbolic Play Test, Early Social Communication Scales, and Parenting Stress Index	not different between the two groups. Language profiles did not change.	

Salt, J., Shemilt, J., Sellars, V., Boyd, S., Coulson, T., & McCool, S. (2002). The Scottish Centre for autism preschool treatment programme II: The results of a controlled treatment outcome study. *Autism, 6,* 34–46.

SOCIAL SKILLS INTERVENTIONS

| Bauminger (2002) | Evaluate the effectiveness of a cognitive behavioral intervention on social–emotional understanding and social interaction in high-functioning children with autism | Level III—One nonrandomized group was measured before and after intervention.

Subjects: Children with autism and verbal IQ of 69 or above; *N* = 15; 4 girls, 11 boys; age range 8.1–17.3 years; study completed in Israel | *Intervention:* Social-emotional curriculum for 3 hours a week for 7 months. The curriculum included: (1) prerequisite concepts, (2) affective education, and (3) social-interpersonal problem solving. Teachers, peers, and parents were involved in promoting the children's social interactions.

Measures: Problem-solving measures, emotion inventory, observation of social interaction, and Social Skills Rating. | After treatment, the group had higher-level problem-solving solutions, more relevant solutions, and fewer nonsocial solutions. Scores on emotions inventory improved. Social skills improved, specifically eye contact, expressing interest, and sharing. On the Social Skills Rating, they improved in cooperation and assertive behavior. | This study did not use a control group; therefore, it is not known if the intervention alone caused the changes. Generalization of social skills in other environments was not measured. Because the evaluators were not blinded to the purpose, ratings may have been biased.

This study has some relevance to occupational therapists who may be interested in implementing part of the curriculum. The findings suggest that a comprehensive, holistic approach is needed. They also suggest that certain aspects of social skills can be learned by children with high-functioning autism. |

Bauminger, N. (2002). The facilitation of social–emotional understanding and social interaction in high-functioning children with autism: Intervention outcomes. *Journal of Autism and Developmental Disorders, 32,* 283–298.

(continued)

Evidence-Based Tables (cont.)

Author/ Year	Study Objectives	Level/Design/ Subjects	Intervention and Outcome Measures	Results	Study Limitations	Implications for Occupational Therapy
Bernard-Opitz et al. (2001)	Research the effectiveness of a computer program in teaching problem solving	Level II—Two groups, nonrandomized. *Subjects:* Children with autism (age range 5.8–8.5 years) and preschool children developing typically (age range 4.0–4.9 years); *N* = 8 in each group	*Intervention:* The computer training gave each child easy and difficult problems to solve. *Measures:* Number of novel ideas, number of appropriate solutions to the problems	Children with autism had a significantly lower number of novel ideas and appropriate solutions. Performance increased over the four probes, so some learning occurred.	This study did not determine if effects from the computer training would generalize to other settings. The sample size was small and not randomly assigned.	Computer programs are one possible adjunct to occupational therapy interventions and may reinforce learning. Children with autism tend to have great interest in computer programs, suggesting that they would participate.

Bernard-Opitz, V., Sriram, N., & Nakhoda-Sapuan, S. (2001). Enhancing social problem solving in children with autism and normal children through computer-assisted instruction. *Journal of Autism and Developmental Disorders, 31,* 377–384.

Broderick et al. (2002)	Examine the effects of a social skills group on adolescents with Asperger syndrome	Level III—Nonrandomized time series design. Students were evaluated before and after, with different baselines. *Subjects:* Adolescents with Asperger syndrome; *N* = 9; 5 began at time 1 and 4 at time 2; no other description of the participants	*Intervention:* Eight sessions of social skills training were provided. Participants were trained in conversational skills, eye contact, body posture, expressing and recognizing nonverbal signals, conflict resolution, and relaxation. Social Stories were used. *Measures:* A self-report on confidence was used. The Piers-Harris Scale was completed before and after.	The participants reported more confidence after the group sessions, and self-esteem measures improved. No statistical analysis was completed. Scores were not reported.	Very small sample size. Nonrandomized. Evaluation was not blinded. Measures seemed inadequate; the report of self-confidence did not show evidence of reliability and validity. Weak evidence given many threats to validity.	Questionable application to occupational therapy given small sample size, weak instrumentation, lack of data analysis, and limitations in research design.

Broderick, C., Caswell, R., Gregory, S., Marzolini, S., & Wilson, O. (2002). "Can I join the club?": A social integration scheme for adolescents with Asperger syndrome. *Autism, 5,* 427–431.

Gevers et al. (2006)	Examine the effectiveness of the theory of mind-based social cognition training on children with PDD–NOS. Theory of mind refers to the ability to	Level III—Nonrandomized before and after group *Subjects: N* = 18 (13 boys, 5 girls); age range 8–11 years; in	*Intervention:* The social cognition training was provided to 5–6 children simultaneously. It included 21 weekly 60-minute sessions, targeted at	The children had significant improvement in TOM scores for perception/imitation, pretense, and irony/humor. They made significant gains in in-	The pre–post design lacked a control group. The sample size was small. The TOM test was a close match to the intervention; therefore,	This study support a theory of mind-based training grounded in social–cognitive theories. Interventions aimed at higher-level thinking

attribute mental states (e.g. beliefs, emotions) to others and to use these in predicting and explaining the behavior of others.

	Netherlands; verbal IQ within normal limits on intelligence testing.	developing theory of mind. The training included 5 monthly sessions of psycho-education of parents about PDD and theory of mind. *Measures:* Theory of Mind (TOM) test; Vineland Adaptive Behavior Scales (VABS)	terpersonal relation-ships, play, and social skills (on VABS). They did not improve in recognition of emotion, understanding of false belief, or distinction of physical and mental.	generalization was not assessed. Long-term effects were not evaluated.	are generally not within the purview of occupational therapy. Given that this is a Level III study with a small sample size, conclusions about the effectiveness of this treatment are premature.

Gevers, C., Clifford, P., Mager, M., & Boer, F. (2006). Brief Report: A theory-of-mind–based social–cognition training program for school-aged children with pervasive developmental disorders: An open study of its effectiveness. *Journal of Autism and Developmental Disorders, 36,* 567–571.

| Howlin & Yates (1999) | Investigate the potential effectiveness of social skills groups for adolescents and adults with autism | Level III—One group before–after study.

Subjects: Male adolescents and adults; *N* = 10; age range 19–44 years, mean 28.4 years | *Intervention:* Social skills group met each month for 2 hours. The focus of the meeting was positive problem solving. Members used role playing, team activities, structured games, and feedback from video recordings of sessions.

Measures: Family reports of sons' social and communication skills; number of participants that left home. Conversation style as rated from videotapes of sessions. | Families reported improvements in social and communication skills. Four of 10 group members left home to live in supported accommodations. Conversational responses improved (became more appropriate). | The intervention appeared not well controlled, but seemed to flow with group interest. The measures were subjective (family report), and reliability/validity were not examined. Without a control group, it is not possible to attribute the change to the intervention. | The social skills groups use many of the principles inherent in occupational therapy, including client-centered activities, building of client choice, use of groups, and emphasis on social skills embedded in occupations. This intervention is one of the few in the research literature designed for adolescents. Although the evidence for positive effects is weak, this intervention is a good fit to occupational therapy. |

Howlin, P., & Yates, P. (1999). The potential effectiveness of social skills group for adults with autism. *Autism, 3,* 299–307.

(continued)

Evidence-Based Tables (cont.)

Author/ Year	Study Objectives	Level/Design/ Subjects	Intervention and Outcome Measures	Results	Study Limitations	Implications for Occupational Therapy
Ozonoff & Miller (1995)	Examine the effectiveness of social skills training on adolescents with autism and normal intelligence	Level II—Non-randomized study with two groups (cohort). *Subjects:* Adolescents with autism; *N* = 9; 5 in the treatment group, 4 in no treatment	*Intervention:* The social skills group met weekly for 4½ months (14 sessions). Social skills were explained, modeled, practiced, and videotaped. The videotapes were reviewed and each child was given feedback. The session focused on interactional and conversational skills, and then perspective taking and theory of mind skills. *Measures:* The Social Skills Rating system was completed by the participant's teacher and parent. Theory of mind tasks were used to determine each participant's ability to take another's perspective.	The adolescents who participated in the social skills training performed marginally better on the theory of mind measures. The treatment group did not demonstrate improvement on the Social Skills Rating system. The researchers concluded that although the adolescents improved on paper-and-pencil tests, their ability to generalize theory of mind to everyday conversation and interactions remained limited.	This study used a very small sample (5 and 4 subjects) that was nonrandomized. The researchers found that theory of mind techniques did not transfer into social skills performance.	This study has limited relevance to occupational therapy because the design is weak. The findings suggest that facilitating development of theory of mind in children with autism may take intense and extensive intervention. Even when the concepts are understood, intervention may be needed to enable generalization to performance.

Ozonoff, S., & Miller, J. (1995). Teaching theory of mind: A new approach to social skills training for individuals with autism. *Journal of Autism and Developmental Disorders, 25,* 415–433.

Author/ Year	Study Objectives	Level/Design/ Subjects	Intervention and Outcome Measures	Results	Study Limitations	Implications for Occupational Therapy
Reynhout & Carter (2006)	Review the empirical research on Social Stories. Social Stories are short stories, often illustrated, that are written to enhance specific behaviors. They are contextually specific, descriptive, directive, and affirmative statements about expected behaviors.	Level I—Systematic review that included both group and single-subject designs *Subjects:* 16 studies were included in the review; the subjects in these studies were generally between 6 and 13 years and had Asperger syndrome,	*Intervention:* Social Stories were used in each of the 16 studies. Social Stories (Gray, 2000) are individually written stories to instruct children to use appropriate behavior. Each story has descriptive, directive, perspective, and affirmative	Nine studies reported an appropriate reduction in targeted behavior, 8 reported an appropriate increase in targeted behaviors, 2 showed no change, and 2 showed an increase in the behavior targeted for extinction. A mean effect size of .99 was	Most of the studies in this review used single-subject design. This is expected, as Social Stories are individual to the child and to targeted behaviors. In some cases, the studies were highly varied in how the stories were constructed and used.	This review suggests that Social Stories have a modest positive effect. Social Stories complement occupational therapy intervention well. They are individualized methods to improve behaviors and functional skills often targeted in occupational therapy

Author/Citation	Purpose	Level/Design/Subjects	Intervention/Measures	Results	Limitations	Comments
		ADHD, autism, Fragile X syndrome, or cognitive delay	Social Stories are read immediately before a child is expected to participate in an activity. statements. The child, a peer, or an adult reads the story before a specific behavior is expected. *Measures:* Each study measured the behaviors targeted in the Social Story. These include social skills, self-care, communication, and negative or disruptive behaviors.	calculated for 3 group studies; the other group studies did not yield an effect size. The 12 single-subject design studies were analyzed by computing a total percentage of nonoverlapping data (PND) between baseline and intervention phases. Using the most valid data, the PND was 51. This mean PND indicates that they are marginally effective. The authors concluded that the effects are modest.	Data were inconsistent across studies. In a number of the studies, Social Stories were combined with other interventions. Questions remain regarding generalizability and whether behaviors are sustained without the Social Story.	cupational therapy intervention. Social Stories are a client-centered approach because the child is a participant in writing and using the story. It is not clear from the results of this study for whom Social Stories are most effective.

Reynhout, G., & Carter, M. (2006). Social Stories for children with disabilities. *Journal of Autism and Developmental Disorders, 36,* 445–469.

Author/Citation	Purpose	Level/Design/Subjects	Intervention/Measures	Results	Limitations	Comments
Smith et al. (2004)	Examine the effectiveness of a shared turn-taking game, emphasizing nonverbal communication on social attention and functional language in children with autism	Level II—Nonrandomized two groups, using within-subjects and across-groups design (crossover design). *Subjects:* Children with autism spectrum disorder (75%) or severe language impairment (25%); *N* = 20; two groups of 10; age range 3–6 years	*Intervention:* Social communication requires joint attention and turn-taking skills in addition to understanding nonverbal and verbal language. This intervention used developmentally appropriate games to establish shared attention, then role exchange through turn-taking to facilitate the child as initiator. Intervention was daily for 6 months with parents carrying out part of the intervention.	Children participated in more complex social interaction roles following intervention. Scores on the WPPSI verbal scale improved dramatically both within groups (baseline to intervention) and between groups (control to intervention). Overall changes in turn-taking and game participation correlated significantly with language scores.	Limitations include a small, nonrandomized sample and lack of explicit description of the intervention or the measures. Lack of detail on who administered the intervention and who tested the children. It appears that measures were not blinded.	This study has limited application to occupational therapy. The focus is language, social interaction, and cognition. This is a British study and may not generalize to U.S. intervention settings. The study is strong on theoretic explanation and weak in explicit description of the methods, limiting the reader's ability to replicate or generalize.

(continued)

Evidence-Based Tables (cont.)

Author/Year	Study Objectives	Level/Design/Subjects	Intervention and Outcome Measures	Results	Study Limitations	Implications for Occupational Therapy
			Measures: Wechsler Preschool and Primary Scale of Intelligence (WPPSI), British Ability Scales, Mean Length of Utterance, Scales of Pragmatic Communication Skills			

Smith, C., Goddard, S., & Fluck, M. (2004). A scheme to promote social attention and functional language in young children with communication difficulties and autistic spectrum disorder. *Educational Psychology in Practice, 20,* 319–334.

COMPREHENSIVE BEHAVIORAL INTERVENTIONS

Author/Year	Study Objectives	Level/Design/Subjects	Intervention and Outcome Measures	Results	Study Limitations	Implications for Occupational Therapy
Bassett et al. (2000)	Examine whether early, intensive behavioral therapy for children with autism results in normal functioning	Level I—Systematic review *Subjects:* Preschool children with autism	*Intervention:* Early (prior to age 5 years) applied behavioral analysis; behavioral therapy; or intensive, home-based programs *Measures:* Intellectual functioning, language, social interaction and play, adaptive or self-care skills, maladaptive behavior	The Lovaas study's claim that Applied Behavior Analysis (ABA) intensive discrete trial training produces normal functioning is misleading because more severely involved children were eliminated. Other published controlled studies do not report children achieving normal functioning. Systematic reviews with critical appraisal fail to find support for Lovaas's effectiveness. Children improve but do not become "normal."	This review attempts to shift the public's belief in the effectiveness of ABA discrete trial training by pointing to numerous studies in which children did not function normally after Lovaas's intervention. It presents quotes from studies, but does not apply typical systematic review methods in coming to an objective conclusion.	This review paints a realistic picture of what benefits children receive from ABA discrete trial training. The intervention demonstrates effectiveness in improving symptoms, skills, and behaviors, but does not remove the diagnosis of autism. The review persuades the consumer to recognize and criticize the rigidity of the ABA approach and to recognize the value of individualized interventions for children.

Bassett, K., Green, C. J., & Kazanjian, A. (2000). *Autism and Lovaas treatment: A systematic review of effectiveness evidence.* Vancouver, BC: Office of Health Technology Assessment.

Author/Year	Study Objectives	Level/Design/Subjects	Intervention and Outcome Measures	Results	Study Limitations	Implications for Occupational Therapy
Cohen et al. (2006)	Replicate the Lovaas study of early intensive behavioral treatment (EIBT) using a community setting	Level II—3-year prospective study comparing two non-randomized groups *Subjects:* Children with autistic spectrum disorder or	*Intervention:* Children in EIBT received 35–40 hours of intensive behavioral treatment (discrete trial training for 3 years). Treatment was provided in home and in peer play	The IQ of the EIBT group increased 25 points, from 62 to 87. The IQ of the comparison group increased 14 points, from 59 to 73. The difference in IQ score	This study was funded by public agencies; therefore, the treatments were provided within public agencies. Parents were able to choose their treatment group.	This study describes EIBT using a model that attempts to help the child integrate into regular education classrooms as the intensive behavioral treatment is faded.

pervasive development disorder not otherwise specified; $N = 42$, 21 (18 boys, 3 girls) in experimental group, 21 (17 boys, 4 girls) age and IQ matched in comparison group; age = 18–42 months at time of entrance into study

training, and included regular education classroom inclusion. After 1 year, the home component began to decrease and the preschool peer play component increased. The intervention was transferred to the classroom with only consultation at home in the final 1 to 2 years. Staff were highly trained and parents were involved at all levels. The comparison group received community-based occupational, physical, and speech therapy with some behavioral therapy, up to 5 hours per week.

Measures: Cognitive function was measured using the Bayley Scales of Infant Development and Merrill Palmer Scale of Mental Tests; language was evaluated using the Reynell Developmental Language Scales; and adaptive behaviors using the Vineland Adaptive Behavior Scales.

was significant; however, differences were not significant on the Merrill Palmer Scale or in expressive language. The groups were significantly different in adaptive behavior and in language comprehension. At year 3, 17 of the 21 EIBT children were in regular education classrooms and 1 of the 21 in the comparison groups was in a regular education classroom. In general, the differences between the EIBT group and the comparison group were smaller than in previous studies.

The evaluators were blind, but also were employed by the center and may have been aware of group identity. Part of the intervention protocol for the EIBT group was to place them in regular education; therefore, it is not surprising that most were in regular education at the end of the study.

This model is more realistic than earlier home-based models and it attempts to meet social goals that were not prioritized in earlier studies. Occupational therapists should encourage the use of models that transition services to preschools and schools in order to help the child learn important social skills and to adjust to school routines. Occupational therapists should consult with behavioral interventionists to develop comprehensive intervention programs.

(continued)

Cohen, H., Amerine-Dickens, M., & Smith, T. (2006). Early intensive behavioral treatment: Replication of the UCLA model in a community setting. *Development and Behavioral Pediatrics,* 27, S145–S155.

Evidence-Based Tables (cont.)

Author/ Year	Study Objectives	Level/Design/ Subjects	Intervention and Outcome Measures	Results	Study Limitations	Implications for Occupational Therapy
Diggle et al. (2006)	Determine the extent to which parent-mediated early intervention has been shown to be effective in treatment of young children with autistic spectrum disorder	Level I—Systematic review *Subjects:* Children ages 1 year to 6 years, 11 months, diagnosed with autism, Asperger syndrome, or pervasive developmental disorder; participants with dual diagnoses could be included	*Interventions:* Included those with significant focus on parents as the mediators. Interventions designed to train parents in managing their child with autism. Training could be group or individual. *Measures:* Child language progress, positive behavior change, parent interaction style. Secondary measures included parent confidence and reduction in parental stress.	Only two studies were identified for inclusion. Children improved in language, which may be due to parents changing their behavior or better understanding their child. Mothers also gained knowledge about autism.	The two studies included were rigorous Level I studies; therefore, the limitations in design and method are few. The two studies were dissimilar and therefore combining results was questionable. This review is limited by the number of studies included.	This review is relevant to occupational therapists because it emphasizes the importance of educating parents and supporting their ability to manage their child's behaviors.

Diggle, T., McConachie, H. R., & Randle, V. R. L. (2006). Parent-mediated early intervention for young children with autism spectrum disorder. *Cochrane Developmental, Psychosocial and Learning Problems Group, Cochrane Database of Systematic Reviews, 1.*

Author/ Year	Study Objectives	Level/Design/ Subjects	Intervention and Outcome Measures	Results	Study Limitations	Implications for Occupational Therapy
Eledevik et al. (2006)	Retrospectively compare children who received low intensity behavioral treatment (12.5 hours/week) to children who received a comparable amount of eclectic treatment	Level II— Nonrandomized controlled study *Subjects:* Children in Norway with autism and mental retardation with ages below 6 years at the start of treatment. The behavioral treatment group had 13 (10 boys, 3 girls) and the comparison group had 15 (14 boys, 1 girl). All participants attended regular kindergarten or elementary school.	*Intervention:* Behavioral treatment was provided through one-on-one teaching, based on the Lovaas protocol. The treatment was provided 12.5 hours per week for a period of 20 months. The eclectic treatment consisted of at least two of the following: alternative communication, applied behavior analysis, total communication, sensorimotor therapies, or TEACCH. This treatment was pro-	The behavioral group showed significantly more change than the eclectic group on intellectual functioning, language comprehension, expressive language, and communication. The groups were not different in daily living skills or adaptive behavior. An 11-point difference in IQ changes when behavior treatment was compared to eclectic produced an effect size of 1.43. Child's	A large margin of error is associated with the small sample size. This was a retrospective study; therefore, the researcher did not control the intervention provided. Records were kept of the interventions each child received, and these were used to categorize the children into groups. Assignment to groups was therefore not random, and parents were involved in deciding what treatment was used.	This study demonstrated that behavior treatment can be effective when provided on a less-intense schedule (12.5 hours/week) than the typical Lovaas protocol (35–40 hours/week). In the eclectic treatment that involved a number of different approaches, the children did not improve, suggesting that combining approaches may be less effective than using one consistent approach.

Citation	Purpose	Methods	Results	Conclusions
		vided 12 hours per week for 20 months. *Measures:* Intelligence using the Bayley Scales of Infant Development, the Standard Binet Intelligence Scale, or the Wechsler Scales; language using the Reynell Developmental Language Scales; adaptive behavior using the Vineland Adaptive Behavior Scales; nonverbal intelligence using the Merrill-Palmer Scales; and pathology scores	level of function at the beginning of the study was predictive of outcome.	Adaptive behavior and social skills did not improve with behavioral treatment, suggesting different treatment approaches are needed to improve these areas.

Eledevik, S., Eikeseth, S., Jahr, E., & Smith, T. (2006). Effects of low-intensity behavioral treatment for children with autism and mental retardation. *Journal of Autism and Developmental Disorders, 36,* 211–224.

Citation	Purpose	Methods	Results	Conclusions
Horner et al. (2002)	Determine the effectiveness of interventions used to reduce problem behaviors, with emphasis on positive behavioral interventions	Level I—Systematic review *Subjects:* Children under 8 years of age with autism and behavioral problems. Five review papers were used in this systematic review. *Intervention:* A variety of interventions were used, including stimulus-based, instruction-based, extinction-based, reinforcement-based, punishment-based, system change, pharmacology, and other. *Measures:* A wide range of measures were used across studies; measures were functional or behavioral assessments.	Aggression/destruction, disruption/tantrums, self-injury, and stereotypy are the behaviors most often targeted in research reports. In a targeted review (within the broader systematic review) using 37 comparisons, in 85% of the comparisons, the tantrums were decreased. In 59%, problem behavior reduction was 90% or greater.	This systematic review focused on problem behaviors. The methods for this review were clearly stated. The studies used were described in a table. The design is strong and provides guidance to future studies. This systematic review provides clinical interpretation useful to practitioners and researchers. Behavioral approaches are emphasized; therefore, most interventions emphasized by occupational therapists to address problem behaviors are not included.

Horner, R., Carr, E., Strain, P., Todd, A., & Reed, H. (2002). Problem behavior interventions for young children. *Journal of Autism and Developmental Disorders, 32,* 423–446.

(continued)

Evidence-Based Tables (cont.)

Author/ Year	Study Objectives	Level/Design/ Subjects	Intervention and Outcome Measures	Results	Study Limitations	Implications for Occupational Therapy
Lovaas (1987)	Investigate the effects of intensive behavior treatment using discrete trial training on young children with autism	Level II—Nonrandomized trial using two groups *Subjects:* Children with autism; *N* = 19 in the treatment group (mean age at beginning, 34.6 months), 19 in the control group (mean age at beginning, 40.9 months); a second control group of 21 children with autism from community programs was included in the analyses	*Intervention:* The intensive treatment group received more than 40 hours of one-on-one home-based treatment per week from trained graduate students. The control group received 10 hours or less of one-on-one treatment per week. The second control group did not receive any treatment designed by the researchers. Duration of treatment was 2 or more years. Goals were continually updated throughout the 2 years. *Measures:* Measures were made when the participants were 7 years. Videotaped recordings of self-stimulatory behavior, appropriate play behaviors, recognizable words, and IQ.	The intensive behavioral treatment group was significantly higher than the two control groups in IQ and educational placement. Nine of the children in the treatment group achieved a normal IQ and were placed in regular education. Eight of the children had IQs in the mildly retarded range and 2 children were in the profoundly retarded range. The intensive treatment group gained a mean of 30 more IQ points than the first control group.	Limitations included nonrandomized assignment and children who were relatively high functioning at the beginning of the study. One limitation of the study is the intensity of the intervention, making it difficult to replicate and to implement practically in schools and the community.	Occupational therapists often work with children who receive (or who have received in the past) intensive behavioral interventions. The occupational therapist's role involves consulting with behavioral specialists regarding play, sensory integration, self-care, motor planning, social-emotional function, and other aspects of the child's performance. Parents and other professionals need to be aware of the research supporting intensive behavioral treatment and the limitations of these studies.

Lovaas, O. (1987). Behavioral treatment and normal educational and intellectual functioning in young autistic children. *Journal of Consultation and Clinical Psychology, 55,* 359–372.

Luiselli et al. (2000)	Evaluate, through retrospective analysis, differences in developmental skills in young children with autism or PDD who received abbreviated home-based behavioral intervention based	Level III—Descriptive follow-up study correlating treatment variables with outcomes; retrospective analysis of one group (children who had received services at the May Center)	*Intervention:* Home-based behavioral therapy based on the methods of Lovaas *Measures:* Service delivery: Hours per week, duration of treatment, total hours of treatment. Outcome	Using regression analyses, only duration of treatment was a predictor of change. Duration predicted communication, cognition, and social-emotional domains. The intensity of treatment did not predict	This small-sample, descriptive study analyzed whether the intensity of behavioral treatment predicts outcome and whether age at which treatment was initiated predicts outcome. Regression equations	This study is of limited application to occupational therapists because they do not develop and direct Lovaas discrete trial training programs. Information from this study can be given to parents who are

	Subjects/Intervention	Results	Comments	
on age treatment was initiated and/or how long treatment was provided	*Subjects:* Children with autism or PDD who received home-based services; *N* = 16; 8 initiated treatment before age 3 years and 8 initiated treatment after age 3 years come: Early Learning Accomplishments Profile (Glover et al., 1998) or Learning Accomplishments Profile (Sanford & Zelman, 1981)	outcomes. The degree of change did not differ between the group that began before 3 years and the group that began after 3 years.	with small samples tend to have error. The only variable that related to more positive outcomes was duration of treatment. Retrospective designs always have limitations in that the intervention is not preconceived and well controlled. Records may not be complete.	considering discrete trial training and have questions about intensity or age to begin. The findings should be disseminated with caution, as the sample was small, and retrospective studies lack the control inherent in clinical trials.

Luiselli, J. K., Cannon, B. O., Ellis, J. T., & Sisson, R. W. (2000). Home-based behavioral intervention for young children with autism/pervasive developmental disorder. *Autism, 4,* 426–438.

McEachie et al. (1993) Follow up the participants of the Lovaas (1987) study at age 13 and examine the children who had the best outcomes	Level II—Follow-up of nonrandomized trial using two groups *Subjects:* Children from the Lovaas study, two groups of 19, were now 10–13 years. The children entered the original study at 3 years but entered sequentially across time, accounting for different ages at this follow-up time.	*Intervention:* One group of the children had participated in the Lovaas program of discrete trial training, 40 hours per week. The control group had a similar treatment 10 hours/week. The 40 hour/week group had participated in a mean of 5 years of treatment and the control group, 3 years. *Measures:* They classified their school placement. They tested IQ using the Wechsler Intelligence Scale for Children–Revised, Leiter International Performance Scale,	Of the 19 children in intensive behavioral intervention, 9 were in regular education classrooms. In the control group, none were in regular education. The intensive behavior treatment group was significantly higher in IQ, with 11 achieving at least an IQ score of 80 and maintaining the gains they had achieved as preschoolers. On the VABS, the treatment group scored significantly higher, and maladaptive behaviors were higher in the control group. The treatment group scored better on the	The follow-up study of Lovaas has the same limitation (i.e., lack of random assignment to the groups). In the follow-up study, the treatment group was older (mean age 13 years) than the control group (mean age 10 years). The analysis was thorough and valid measures were used.	Occupational therapists need to be familiar with the research evidence for behavioral treatments as they treat children who also receive behavioral interventions and/or participate in behavioral intervention. The findings of Lovaas and McEachie and colleagues had widespread ramifications that led to wide use of ABA discrete trial training programs and great family interest in obtaining this treatment for their children. Limitations of the treatment are the intensive resources and

(continued)

Evidence-Based Tables (cont.)

Author/ Year	Study Objectives	Level/Design/ Subjects	Intervention and Outcome Measures	Results	Study Limitations	Implications for Occupational Therapy
McEachie et al. (1993) (cont.)			and/or the Peabody Picture Vocabulary Test—Revised. They rated adapted behavior using the Vineland Adaptive Behavior Scales and used the Personality Inventory for Children. Blinded evaluation was used.	Personality Functioning measure. Of the 9 children who had achieved normal functioning in the original study, 8 continued to exhibit average intelligence.		time demands, and difficulties in implementing the program in school and community programs.

McEachie, J. J., Smith, T., & Lovaas, O. (1993). Long-term outcome for children with autism who received early intensive behavioral treatment. *American Journal of Mental Retardation, 97,* 350–372.

Author/ Year	Study Objectives	Level/Design/ Subjects	Intervention and Outcome Measures	Results	Study Limitations	Implications for Occupational Therapy
Sallows & Graupner (2005)	Examine if a community-based program achieves similar results to the studies by Lovaas (using discrete trial training); examine residual symptoms of autism in children who receive discrete trial training; and examine effectiveness of a parent-directed treatment model	Level I—Randomized controlled trial. Children were randomly assigned to a clinic-directed group or a parent-directed group. *Subjects:* The clinic-directed group had 13 (11 boys, 2 girls) and the parent-directed group had 10 (8 boys, 2 girls)	*Intervention:* All children received treatment based on the Lovaas discrete trial training model. Children in the clinical group received 40 hours per week of direct treatment in the home, of which 6–10 hours was supervised by a senior therapist. In the parent-directed group, children averaged 32 hours of direct intervention in their homes. The parents had substantially less supervision. *Measures:* Bayley Scales of Infant Development, Merrill Palmer Scale of Mental Tests, Reynell Developmental Language Scales, Wechsler Preschool and Primary Scale of Intelligence, Wechsler Intelligence Scale for Children to the Out-	The average IQ for all 23 children increased from 51 to 76, a 25 point increase. Eleven of 23 children achieved full-scale IQs in the average range. There were no significant differences between groups (parent directed, clinic) at pre- or posttest. Eleven of the 23 demonstrated extraordinarily rapid and significant change. Variables that predicted positive outcomes were full-scale IQ, language, and social skills. Imitation skills also predicted outcome.	One limitation is that this study was 4 years in length, which may have introduced interfering variables. The pretest (Bayley) may have been different from the posttest (Wechsler). This study was well designed and well analyzed.	This study has relevance for occupational therapists because it is a well-designed study demonstrating the powerful effects of discrete trial training. A major significant issue is that the treatment was provided 32–40 hours a week, which is a huge cost for families.

Sallows, G. O., & Graupner, T. D. (2005). Intensive behavioral treatment for children with autism: Four-year outcome and predictors. *American Journal on Mental Retardation, 110,* 417–438.

come Measures, Vineland Adaptive Behavior Scales, IQ, the Early Learning Measures

Study	Purpose	Design/Subjects	Intervention/Measures	Results	Comments	Relevance
Smith et al. (2000)	Examine the effectiveness of Lovaas discrete trial training using a less intensive protocol than the original and include children with PDD–NOS	Level I—Randomized controlled trial. *Subjects:* Children with autism or PDD–NOS from the UCLA Young Autism Project; *N* = 28; mean age 36 months; 15 (12 males, 3 females) in the intensive treatment group and 13 (11 males, 2 females) in the parent training group	*Intervention:* The intensive treatment group received discrete trial training 30 hours per week that was phased out after 18 months. In the parent training group, the children's families receive 2 sessions (5 hours per week) of parent training for 3 to 9 months. Parents were asked to work with their children 5 hours per week (in addition to the 5 hours with the trainer). *Measures:* Stanford Binet Intelligence Scale, Bayley Scales of Infant Development, Merrill Palmer Scale of Mental Tests, Reynell Language Tests, Vineland Adaptive Behavior Scales, Achenbach Child Behavior Checklist, Weschler Individualized Achievement Test (WIAT), Early Learning Measure, and family satisfaction.	At follow-up testing, the intensive treatment group was statistically higher in IQ, visual–spatial skills, and language development, but not in adaptive behavior. The intensively treated group had less restrictive school placement and higher WIAT. Changes on the Child Behavior Checklist were not significantly different. Family satisfaction was high for both groups.	This study was well designed and well implemented. It used random assignment and blind evaluators. The sample size is relatively small, as would be expected in a long-term trial. This study is important because it replicates previous positive results of Lovaas training.	This study is relevant to occupational therapy because it is well designed with few threats to validity. Intensive treatment (30 hours per week) produces positive changes in children's behavior and development. These positive findings place occupational therapists in a dilemma, because current service delivery systems do not allow for such intensive services. Discrete trial training appears to have positive effects; it also is extremely costly in terms of manpower and resources required to implement.

Smith, T., Groen, A. D., & Wynn, J. W. (2000). Randomized trial of intensive early intervention for children with pervasive developmental disorder. *American Journal on Mental Retardation, 105,* 269–285.

(continued)

Evidence-Based Tables (cont.)

Author/ Year	Study Objectives	Level/Design/ Subjects	Intervention and Outcome Measures	Results	Study Limitations	Implications for Occupational Therapy
Smith et al. (2002)	Evaluate behavioral treatment of children with autism when paired with typical peers as compared to behavioral treatment when children were paired with peers with developmental delays	Level II—Nonrandomized within group (children served as their own control; within subjects, crossover design). Behaviors of children with high-functioning autism paired with peers with developmental delay were compared to behaviors when paired with peers who were developing typically. *Subjects:* Children with autism who received 40 hours per week of discrete trial training (N = 9; age range 58–88 months); children developing typically who had no known developmental delays (N = 9; age range 52–93 months); children with delays who had IQ scores lower than 70 (N = 9; age range 68–97 months)	*Intervention:* Each child participated in 2 15-minute sessions in each of two conditions, with a peer developing typically in an integrated condition and with a peer with developmental delays in a segregated condition. The four sessions were counterbalanced. *Measures:* The children were videotaped and behaviors rated were: (1) interactive toy play, (2) interactive speech, (3) solitary toy play, (4) solitary speech, and (5) self-stimulatory behavior. Examiners had high (90%) agreement on scores.	Children with autism had significantly more interactive play and speech in the integrated condition than in the segregated condition. They displayed less self-stimulation. The frequency of solitary play and speech did not differ between conditions. These differences were consistent across the children.	A small nonrandomized sample was used. The two conditions were each 30 minutes in duration, so the results cannot be viewed as definitive. Despite the short duration, the results were significant. This study provides data on behavior that validate clinical perceptions that behaviors of children with autism are more appropriate and interactive with peers developing typically than with peers with delays.	This study reinforces the notion of integrated classrooms. It suggests that behaviors of children with autism may be at a higher level simply through the natural modeling that occurs when they are paired with children who are developing typically. These pairings also may be beneficial because typical children can initiate and reinforce the play of others. Although the sample was small and the independent variable was of short duration, the results do have implications for occupational therapists, suggesting that they should include typical children when they implement intervention in groups.

Smith, T., Lovaas, N. W., & Lovaas, O. I. (2002). Behaviors of children with high-functioning autism when paired with typically developing versus delayed peers: A preliminary study. *Behavioral Interventions, 17,* 129–143.

Sofronoff & Farbotko (2002)	Evaluate the effectiveness of parent management training on self-efficacy in parents of children with Asperger syndrome	Level II—Three groups, nonrandomized. One group of parents attended a workshop, one attended individual sessions, one did not attend any parent training.	*Intervention:* Parent management training was implemented. This training encourages parents to become actively involved in interventions that strengthen family functioning.	Parent self-efficacy and child behaviors were significantly different from time 1 to time 2 and time 1 to time 3 (follow-up). Child behavior differed significantly when trained groups	Sample assessment was nonrandomized. Description of the intervention was minimal. Self-report measures were used, and the parent self-efficacy measure appears not standard-	Parent management training can improve both parent self-efficacy and child behaviors. Parent groups are an important complement to occupational therapy treatment and may be

Author (Year)	Purpose	Design/Subjects	Methods	Results	Comments	Conclusions
		Subjects: Parents of children (6–12 years) with Asperger syndrome in Australia; N = 99; 45 mothers, 44 fathers; 33 in workshop, 26 in individual sessions, and 20 in a wait list control group	The intervention was provided in a 1-day workshop or in 6 weekly individual sessions. Both formats were compared to a control group. Measures: A questionnaire: "Parental self-efficacy in the management of Asperger syndrome" and the Eyberg Child Behaviour Inventory; measures were administered at the beginning, 4 weeks after the training, and 3 months later.	were compared to the control group. Parent self-efficacy did not differ among the three groups, although there was a significant time-by-group interaction when the three groups were compared. Effects in self-efficacy were greater for mothers than fathers.	ized. Reliability and validity of this measure are not reported, and it appears to be unpublished. The control group was lost after the second measure.	run by occupational therapists. Parent training is essential when the child's behaviors are disruptive or difficult to manage. When child behavior and parent self-efficacy are issues, occupational therapists should consider referring parents to and/or running parent management groups.

Sofronoff, K., & Farbotko, M. (2002). The effectiveness of parent management training to increase self-efficacy in parents of children with Asperger syndrome. *Autism, 6,* 271–286.

Author (Year)	Purpose	Design/Subjects	Methods	Results	Comments	Conclusions
Sofronoff et al. (2004)	Evaluate the effects of parent management training on reduction of the number and intensity of problem behaviors reported by parents of children with Asperger syndrome; evaluate different methods of delivery of the training modules to parents	Level I—Three groups, randomly assigned. Subjects: Parents with a primary school–age child recently diagnosed with Asperger syndrome; N = 51; child age range 6–12 years (mean age 9.4 years).	Intervention: Parents attended a workshop on parent management or participated in six 1-hour sessions. The control group was on a waiting list. Measures: The Eyberg Child Behaviour Inventory, Social Skills Questionnaire, and a usefulness questionnaire	Both intervention methods resulted in reduction of problem behaviors immediately after the training and at follow-up. Intensity of behaviors decreased the most in the group who participated in the six sessions. Social skills improved in the groups who received training. The parents reported that the training was very helpful.	The sample size was small. The parents were not blinded to the treatment and may have been biased in completing the evaluations. All measures used parent report.	This study suggests that parent training in managing behavior can be effective in reducing problem behaviors. Occupational therapy can support parent management of behavior using similar methods of parent training (e.g., Gray's Social Stories, Comic Strip Conversations).

Sofronoff, K., Leslie, A., & Brown, W. (2004). Parent management training and Asperger syndrome. *Autism, 8,* 301–317.

Appendix E.
Selected *CPT*^{TM} Coding for Occupational Therapy Evaluations and Interventions

The following chart can guide making clinically appropriate decisions in selecting the most relevant *CPT*^{TM} code to describe occupational therapy evaluation and intervention. Occupational therapy practitioners should use the most appropriate code from the current *CPT* based on specific services provided, individual patient goals, payer policy, and common usage.

Examples of Occupational Therapy Evaluation and Intervention	Suggested *CPT*^{TM} Code(s)
Evaluation	
Evaluate/assess changes in such areas as • Play, school, and adaptive occupations • Motor performance and sensory processing skills necessary for play, school, and adaptive occupations	97003—Occupational therapy evaluation. 97004—Occupational therapy reevaluation. 97750—Physical performance test or measurement (e.g., musculoskeletal, functional capacity), with written report, each 15 minutes.
Administration of standardized assessments like • PDMS–2 or BOT–2 as part of the motor assessment • PEDI, Vineland, or SIB–R as part of the adaptive assessment	96110—Developmental testing; limited (e.g., Developmental Screening Test II, Early Language Milestone Screen) with interpretation and report. 96111—Developmental testing extended (includes assessment of motor, language, social, adaptive, and/or cognitive functioning by standardized developmental instruments) with interpretation and report.
Participation in a team conference as part of a diagnostic team in which the team conveys evaluation findings, diagnoses, and recommendations to a client's family	99366—Medical team conference with an interdisciplinary team of health care professionals, face-to-face with patient and/or family, 30 minutes or more, participation by non-physician qualified health care professional.
Participation in a team conference as part of a diagnostic team in which the team reviews evaluation findings and clarifies diagnostic considerations and recommendations prior to meeting with a client's family	99368—Medical team conference with an interdisciplinary team of health care professionals, patient and/or family not present, 30 minutes or more, participation by non-physician qualified health care professional.
Intervention	
Provide functional exercises to increase range of motion, strength, and mobility to enhance participation in daily activities	97110—Therapeutic procedure, one or more areas, each 15 minutes; therapeutic exercises to develop strength and endurance, range of motion and flexibility. 97113—Aquatic therapy with therapeutic exercises.

(continued)

Examples of Occupational Therapy Evaluation and Intervention	Suggested *CPT*™ Code(s)
Design graded activities to increase coordination, balance, and sensory awareness to enhance participation in daily occupations	97112—Neuromuscular reeducation of movement, balance, coordination, kinesthetic sense, posture, and/or proprioception for sitting and/or standing activities.
Design and implementation of therapeutic social skill or sensorimotor groups to individuals with an autism spectrum disorder	97150—Therapeutic procedure(s), group (2 or more individuals) (group therapy procedures involve constant attendance of the physician or therapist but by definition do not require one-on-one patient contact by the physician or therapist).
Design interventions to improve or train in compensatory strategies for positioning, adaptive equipment, and food texture or appearance to maximize oral intake for enhanced nutritional status	92526—Treatment of swallowing dysfunction and/or oral function for feeding.
Design and implementation of occupation-based activities to facilitate participation in and performance of play, school, and adaptive occupations	97530—Therapeutic activities, direct one-on-one patient contact by the provider (use of dynamic activities to improve functional performance), each 15 minutes.
Design and implementation of sensory integrative interventions to facilitate adaptive responding and optimal arousal to allow for enhanced participation in play, school, and adaptive occupations	97533—Sensory integrative techniques to enhance sensory processing and promote adaptive responses to environmental demands, direct one-on-one patient contact by the provider, each 15 minutes.
Provide instruction and intervention to improve participation and performance in adaptive/self-care activities. May include training in compensatory techniques for performing self-care tasks.	97535—Self-care home management training (e.g., activities of daily living and compensatory training, meal preparation, safety procedures, and instruction in use of assistive technology devices/adaptive equipment), direct one-on-one contact by the provider, each 15 minutes.
Provide activities and training for • Social aspects of the workplace (e.g., greeting coworkers, conversation) • Specific job tasks • Social aspects of occupations performed in community setting (e.g., ordering food and eating in a restaurant, grocery shopping)	97537—Community/work reintegration training (e.g., shopping, transportation, money management, avocational activities, and/or work environment/modification analysis, work task analysis, use of assistive technology device/adaptive equipment), direct one-on-one contact by the provider, each 15 minutes.

Source. Adapted from American Medical Association. (2008). *CPT 2009 professional edition* (pp. 433, 439–442). Chicago: Author.

Note. The *CPT 2008* codes referenced in this document do not represent all of the possible codes that may be used in occupational therapy evaluation and intervention. Not all payers will reimburse for all codes. Refer to *CPT 2009* for the complete list of available codes.

CPT™ is a trademark of the American Medical Association (AMA). *CPT* five-digit codes, nomenclature, and other data are copyright 2008 by the American Medical Association. All rights reserved. No fee schedules, basic units, relative values, or related listings are included in *CPT*. The AMA assumes no liability for the data contained herein. Codes shown refer to *CPT 2009*. *CPT* codes are updated annually. New and revised codes become effective January 1. Always refer to the annual updated *CPT* publication for most current codes.

Appendix F.
Preparation and Qualifications of Occupational Therapists and Occupational Therapy Assistants

Who Are Occupational Therapists?

To practice as an occupational therapist, the individual trained in the United States

- Has graduated from an occupational therapy program accredited by the Accreditation Council for Occupational Therapy Education (ACOTE®) or predecessor organizations;
- Has successfully completed a period of supervised fieldwork experience required by the recognized educational institution where the applicant met the academic requirements of an educational program for occupational therapists that is accredited by ACOTE or predecessor organizations;
- Has passed a nationally recognized entry-level examination for occupational therapists; and
- Fulfills state requirements for licensure, certification, or registration.

Educational Programs for the Occupational Therapist

These include the following:
- Biological, physical, social, and behavioral sciences
- Basic tenets of occupational therapy
- Occupational therapy theoretical perspectives
- Screening and evaluation
- Formulation and implementation of an intervention plan
- Context of service delivery
- Management of occupational therapy services (master's level)
- Leadership and management (doctoral level)
- Use of research
- Professional ethics, values, and responsibilities.

The fieldwork component of the program is designed to develop competent, entry-level, generalist occupational therapists by providing experience with a variety of clients across the life span and in a variety of settings. Fieldwork is integral to the program's curriculum design and includes an in-depth experience in delivering occupational therapy services to clients, focusing on the application of purposeful and meaningful occupation and/or research, administration, and management of occupational therapy services. The fieldwork experience is designed to promote clinical reasoning and reflective practice, to transmit the values and beliefs that enable ethical practice, and to develop professionalism and competence in career responsibilities. Doctoral-level students must also complete a doctoral experiential component designed to develop advanced skills beyond a generalist level.

Who Are Occupational Therapy Assistants?

To practice as an occupational therapy assistant, the individual trained in the United States

- Has graduated from an occupational therapy assistant program accredited by ACOTE or predecessor organizations;
- Has successfully completed a period of supervised fieldwork experience required by the recognized

educational institution where the applicant met the academic requirements of an educational program for occupational therapy assistants that is accredited by ACOTE or predecessor organizations;

- Has passed a nationally recognized entry-level examination for occupational therapy assistants; and
- Fulfills state requirements for licensure, certification, or registration.

Educational Programs for the Occupational Therapy Assistant

These include the following:
- Biological, physical, social, and behavioral sciences
- Basic tenets of occupational therapy
- Screening and assessment
- Intervention and implementation
- Context of service delivery
- Assistance in management of occupational therapy services
- Professional literature
- Professional ethics, values, and responsibilities.

The fieldwork component of the program is designed to develop competent, entry-level, generalist occupational therapy assistants by providing experience with a variety of clients across the life span and in a variety of settings. Fieldwork is integral to the program's curriculum design and includes an in-depth experience in delivering occupational therapy services to clients, focusing on the application of purposeful and meaningful occupation. The fieldwork experience is designed to promote clinical reasoning appropriate to the occupational therapy assistant role, to transmit the values and beliefs that enable ethical practice, and to develop professionalism and competence in career responsibilities.

Regulation of Occupational Therapy Practice

All occupational therapists and occupational therapy assistants must practice under federal and state law. Currently, 50 states, the District of Columbia, Puerto Rico, and Guam have enacted laws regulating the practice of occupational therapy.

Note. The majority of this information is taken from the *Accreditation Standards for a Doctoral-Degree-Level Educational Program for the Occupational Therapist* (AOTA, 2007a), *Accreditation Standards for a Master's-Degree-Level Educational Program for the Occupational Therapist* (AOTA, 2007b), and *Accreditation Standards for an Educational Program for the Occupational Therapy Assistant* (AOTA, 2007c).

■ ■ ■

References

Abidin, R. (1995). *Parent Stress Index (PSI) manual* (3rd ed.). Lutz, FL: Psychological Assessment Resources.

Achenbach, T. M., & Rescorla, L. A. (2001). *Manual for the ASEBA school-age forms and profiles.* Burlington: University of Vermont, Research Center for Children, Youth, and Families.

Adams, L. (1998). Oral–motor and motor–speech characteristics of children with autism. *Focus on Autism and Other Developmental Disorders, 13,* 108–112.

Adrien, J. L., Lenoir, P., Martineau, J., Perrot, A., Hameury, L., Larmande, C., et al. (1993). Blind ratings of early symptoms of autism based upon home movies. *Journal of the American Academy of Child and Adolescent Psychiatry, 32,* 617–626.

Adrien, J. L., Ornitz, E., Barthelemy, C., Sauvage, D., & Lelord, G. (1987). The presence or absence of certain behaviors associated with infantile autism in severely retarded autistic and nonautistic retarded children and very young normal children. *Journal of Autism and Developmental Disorders, 17,* 407–416.

Adrien, J. L., Perrot, A., Sauvage, D., Leddet, I., Larmande, C., Hameury, L., et al. (1992). Early symptoms in autism from family home movies. *Acta Paedopsychiatrica, 55,* 71–75.

Alpern, C. S., & Zager, D. (2007). Addressing communication needs for young adults with autism in a college-based inclusion program. *Education and Training in Developmental Disabilities, 42,* 428–436.

Aman, M. G. (2005). Treatment planning for patients with autism spectrum disorders. *Journal of Clinical Psychiatry, 66*(Suppl. 10), 38–45.

American Medical Association. (2008). *CPT 2009.* Chicago: Author.

American Occupational Therapy Association. (1979). *Occupational therapy product output reporting system and uniform terminology for reporting occupational therapy services.* (Available from American Occupational Therapy Association, 4720 Montgomery Lane, Bethesda, MD 20814)

American Occupational Therapy Association. (1989). *Uniform terminology for occupational therapy* (2nd ed.). (Available from American Occupational Therapy Association, 4720 Montgomery Lane, Bethesda, MD 20814)

American Occupational Therapy Association. (1994). Uniform terminology for occupational therapy (3rd ed.). *American Journal of Occupational Therapy, 48,* 1047–1054.

American Occupational Therapy Association. (2002). Occupational therapy practice framework: Domain and process. *American Journal of Occupational Therapy, 56,* 609–639.

American Occupational Therapy Association. (2005). Standards of practice for occupational therapy. *American Journal of Occupational Therapy, 59,* 663–665.

American Occupational Therapy Association. (2006). Policy 1.44: Categories of occupational therapy personnel. In *Policy manual* (2007 ed., pp. 33–34). Bethesda, MD: Author.

American Occupational Therapy Association. (2007a). Accreditation standards for a doctoral-degree-level educational program for the occupational therapist. *American Journal of Occupational Therapy, 61,* 641–651.

American Occupational Therapy Association. (2007b). Accreditation standards for master's-degree-level educational program for the occupational therapist. *American Journal of Occupational Therapy, 61,* 652–661.

American Occupational Therapy Association. (2007c). Accreditation standards for an educational program for the occupational therapy assistant. *American Journal of Occupational Therapy, 61,* 662–671.

American Occupational Therapy Association. (2008a). Guidelines for documentation of occupational therapy. *American Journal of Occupational Therapy, 62,* 684–690.

American Occupational Therapy Association. (2008b). Occupational therapy practice framework: Domain and process (2nd ed.). *American Journal of Occupational Therapy, 62,* 625–683.

American Occupational Therapy Association. (2009). Guidelines for supervision, roles, and responsibilities during the delivery of occupational therapy services. *American Journal of Occupational Therapy, 63.*

American Psychiatric Association. (1980). *Diagnostic and statistical manual of mental disorders* (3rd ed.). Washington, DC: Author.

American Psychiatric Association. (1987). *Diagnostic and statistical manual of mental disorders* (3rd ed., rev.). Washington, DC: Author.

American Psychiatric Association. (1994). *Diagnostic and statistical manual of mental disorders* (4th ed.). Washington, DC: Author.

American Psychiatric Association. (2001). *Diagnostic and statistical manual of mental disorders* (4th ed., rev.). Washington, DC: Author.

Amundson, M. (1995). *Evaluation Tool of Children's Handwriting.* Homer, AK: OT Kids.

Asperger, H. (1944). Die "autistischen psychpathen" im kindesalter. *Arch Psychiatric Nervenkr, 117,* 76–136.

Audet, L. R., Mann, D. J., & Miller-Kuhaneck, H. (2004). Occupational therapy and speech–language pathology: Collaboration within transdisciplinary teams to improve communication in children with an autism spectrum disorder. In H. Miller-Kuhaneck (Ed.), *Autism: A comprehensive occupational therapy approach* (2nd ed., pp. 275–308). Bethesda, MD: AOTA Press.

Autism Society of America. (2008). *What is autism?* Retrieved February 2, 2008, from http://www.autism-society.org/site/PageServer?pagename=about_whatis

Ayres, A. J. (1979). *Sensory integration and the child.* Los Angeles: Western Psychological Services.

Ayres, A. J. (1989). *Sensory Integration and Praxis Tests.* Los Angeles: Western Psychological Services.

Ayres, A. J., & Tickle, L. (1980). Hyperresponsivity to touch and vestibular stimuli as a predictor of positive response to sensory integration procedures in autistic children. *American Journal of Occupational Therapy, 34,* 375–381.

Bailey, D. B., Mesibov, G. B., Hatton, D. D., Clark, R. D., Roberts, J. E., & Mayhew, L. (1998). Autistic behavior in young boys with Fragile X syndrome. *Journal of Autism and Developmental Disorders, 28,* 499–508.

Bailey, A., Phillips, W., & Rutter, M. (1996). Autism: Toward an integration of clinical, genetic, neuropsychological, and neurobiological perspectives. *Journal of Child Psychology and Psychiatry and Allied Disciplines, 37,* 89–126.

Baranek, G. T. (1999). Autism during infancy: A retrospective video analysis of sensory–motor and social behaviors at 9–12 months of age. *Journal of Autism and Developmental Disorders, 29,* 213–224.

Baranek, G. T. (2002). Effectiveness of sensory and motor interventions in autism. *Journal of Autism and Developmental Disorders, 32,* 397–422.

Baranek, G. T., Foster, L. G., & Berkson, G. (1997). Tactile defensiveness and stereotypic behaviors. *American Journal of Occupational Therapy, 51,* 91–95.

Bassett, K., Green, C. J., & Kazanjian, A. (2000). *Autism and Lovaas treatment: A systematic review of effectiveness evidence.* Vancouver, BC: Office of Health Technology Assessment.

Bauman, M. L. (1999). Autism: Clinical features and neurobiological observations. In H. Tager-Flusberg (Ed.), *Neurodevelopmental disorders* (pp. 383–400). Cambridge, MA: Bradford.

Bauman, M. L., & Kemper, T. L. (2004). *The neurobiology of autism* (2nd ed.). Baltimore: Johns Hopkins Press.

Bauminger, N. (2002). The facilitation of social–emotional understanding and social interaction in high-functioning children with autism: Intervention outcomes. *Journal of Autism and Developmental Disorders, 32,* 283–298.

Bayley, N. (2005). *Bayley Scales of Infant Development* (3rd ed.). San Antonio, TX: Psychological Corporation.

Beery, K. E., Buktenica, N. A., & Beery, N. A. (2004). *Beery–Buktenica Developmental Test of Visual–Motor Integration (VMI)* (5th ed.). Parsippany, NJ: Modern Curriculum Press.

Bennetto, L., Pennington, B. F., & Rogers, S. J. (1996). Intact and impaired memory functions in autism. *Child Development, 67,* 1816–1835.

Bernard-Opitz, V., Sriram, N., & Nakhoda-Sapuan, S. (2001). Enhancing social problem solving in children with autism and normal children through computer-assisted instruction. *Journal of Autism and Developmental Disorders, 31,* 377–384.

Bettelheim, B. (1967). *The empty fortress: Infantile autism and the birth of the self.* Oxford: Free Press of Glencoe.

Bettison, S. (1996). The long-term effects of auditory training on children with autism. *Journal of Autism and Developmental Disorders, 26,* 361–375.

Blanche, E. (2002). *Observations based on sensory integration theory.* Los Angeles: Western Psychological Corporation.

Bleuler, E. (1911, tr. 1950). [*Dementia Praecox.*] (J. Zinkin, Trans.). New York: International Universities Press.

Broderick, C., Caswell, R., Gregory, S., Marzolini, S., & Wilson, O. (2002). "Can I join the club?": A social integration scheme for adolescents with Asperger syndrome. *Autism, 5,* 427–431.

Bruininks, R. H., & Bruininks, B. D. (2005). *Bruininks–Oseretsky Test of Motor Proficiency* (2nd ed.). Circle Pines, MN: AGS.

Bruininks, R. H., Woodcock, R. W., Weatherman, R. F., & Hill, B. K. (1997). *Scales of Independent Behavior* (rev.). Itasca, IL: Riverside.

Bryson, S., Rogers, S., & Fombonne, E. (2003). Autism spectrum disorders: Early detection, intervention, education, and psychopharmacological management. *Canadian Journal of Psychiatry, 48,* 506–516.

Bundy, A., Lane, S., & Murray, E. (Eds.). (2002). *Sensory integration: Theory and practice* (2nd ed.). Philadelphia: F. A. Davis.

Buxbaum, J. D. (2005). The genetics of autism spectrum disorders. *Medscape Psychiatry and Mental Health, 10*(2). Retrieved September 16, 2007, from http://www.medscape.com/viewarticle/520013

Case-Smith, J., & Bryan, T. (1999). The effects of occupational therapy with sensory integration emphasis on preschool-age children with autism. *American Journal of Occupational Therapy, 53,* 489–497.

Case-Smith, J., & Miller, H. (1999). Occupational therapy with children with pervasive developmental disorder. *American Journal of Occupational Therapy, 53,* 506–513.

Centers for Disease Control and Prevention. (2007a). Prevalence of autism spectrum disorders—Autism and Developmental Disabilities Monitoring Network, 6 sites, United States, 2000. *MMWR Surveillance Summaries, 56,* 1–11.

Centers for Disease Control and Prevention. (2007b). Prevalence autism spectrum disorders—Autism and

Developmental Disabilities Monitoring Network, 14 sites, United States, 2002. *MMWR Surveillance Summaries, 56,* 12–28.

Cesaroni, L., & Garber, M. (1991). Exploring the experience of autism through firsthand accounts. *Journal of Autism and Developmental Disorders, 21,* 303–313.

Charman, T., Swettenham, J., & Baron-Cohen, S. (1997). Infants with autism: An investigation of empathy, pretend play, joint attention, and imitation. *Developmental Psychology, 33,* 781–789.

Cohen, H., Amerine-Dickens, M., & Smith, T. (2006). Early intensive behavioral treatment: Replication of the UCLA model in a community setting. *Development and Behavioral Pediatrics, 27,* S145–S155.

Colarusso, R. P., & Hammill, D. D. (2003). *Motor-Free Visual Perception Test* (3rd ed.). Novato, CA: Academic Therapy Publications.

Constantino, J. N., & Gruber, C. P. (2005). *The Social Responsiveness Scale.* Los Angeles: Psychological Corporation.

Cook, D. (1991). The assessment process. In W. Dunn (Ed.), *Pediatric occupational therapy: Facilitating effective service provision* (pp. 35–72). Thorofare, NJ: Slack.

Cornish, K. M., & McManus, I. C. (1996). Hand preference and hand skill in children with autism. *Journal of Autism and Developmental Disorders, 26,* 597–609.

Coster, W., Deeney, T., Haltiwanger, J., & Haley, S. (1998). *The School Function Assessment.* San Antonio, TX: Psychological Corporation.

Dahlgren, S. O., & Gillberg, C. (1989). Symptoms in the first two years of life: A preliminary population study of infantile autism. *European Archives of Psychology and Neurological Sciences, 238,* 169–174.

Dawson, G., & Galpert, L. (1990). Mothers' use of initiative play for facilitating social responsiveness and toy play in young autistic children. *Development and Psychopathology, 2,* 151–162.

Dawson, G., & Lew, A. (1989). Arousal, attention, and socioeconomical impairments of individuals with autism. In G. Dawson (Ed.), *Autism: Nature, diagnosis and treatment* (pp. 49–74). New York: Guilford Press.

Dawson, G., Meltzoff, A. N., Osterling, J., & Rinaldi, J. (1998). Neuropsychological correlates of early symptom in autism. *Child Development, 69,* 1276–1285.

Dawson, G., & Osterling, J. (1997). Early intervention in autism. In M. Guralnick (Ed.), *The effectiveness of early intervention* (pp. 307–326). Baltimore: Paul H. Brookes.

Dawson, G., & Watling, R. (2000). Interventions to facilitate auditory, visual, and motor integration in autism: A review of the evidence. *Journal of Autism and Developmental Disorders, 30,* 415–421.

de Kruif, R. E. L., & McWilliam, R. A. (1999). Multivariate relationships among developmental age, global engagement, and observed child engagement. *Early Childhood Research Quarterly, 14,* 515–536.

DeMyer, M. K. (1976). Motor, perceptual–motor, and intellectual disabilities in autistic children. In L. Wing (Ed.), *Early childhood autism* (2nd ed., pp. 169–196). Elmsford, NY: Pergamon Press.

DeMyer, M. K., Hingtgen, J. N., & Jackson, R. K. (1981). Infantile autism reviewed: A decade of research. *Schizophrenia Bulletin, 7,* 388–451.

DiCicco-Bloom, E., Lord, C., Zwaigenbaum, L., Courchesne, E., Dager, S. R., Schmitz, C., et al. (2006). The developmental neurobiology of autism spectrum disorder. *Journal of Neuroscience, 26,* 6897–6906.

Diggle, T., McConachie, H. R., & Randle, V. R. L. (2006). Parent-mediated early intervention for young children with autism spectrum disorder. *Cochrane Developmental, Psychosocial and Learning Problems Group, Cochrane Database of Systematic Reviews, 1.*

Dunlap, G. (1999). Consensus, engagement, and family involvement for young children with autism. *Journal of the Association for Persons With Severe Handicaps, 24,* 222–225.

Dunn, W. (1994). Performance of typical children on the Sensory Profile: An item analysis. *American Journal of Occupational Therapy, 48,* 967–974.

Dunn, W. (1997). The impact of sensory processing on the daily lives of young children and their families: A conceptual model. *Infants and Young Children, 9,* 23–35.

Dunn, W. (1999). *The Sensory Profile: User's manual.* San Antonio, TX: Psychological Corporation.

Dunn, W., & Westman, K. (1997). The Sensory Profile: Performance from a national sample of children without disabilities. *American Journal of Occupational Therapy, 51,* 25–34.

Dunst, C., Hamby, D., Trivett, C. M., Raab, M., & Bruder, M. B. (2000). Everyday family and community life and children's naturally occurring learning opportunities. *Journal of Early Intervention, 23,* 151–164.

Easter Seals. (2008). *Living with autism study.* Retrieved March 13, 2009, from http://www.easterseals.com/site/PageServer?pagename=ntlc8_living_with_autism_study_home&s_src=autism_study&amps;s_subscr=homepage

Edelson, S. M., Arin, D., Bauman, M., Lucas, S. E., Rudy, J. H., Sholar, M., et al. (1999). Auditory integration training: A double-blind study of behavioral and electrophysiological effects in people with autism. *Focus on Autism and Other Developmental Disabilities, 14,* 73–81.

Edelson, S. M., Edelson, M. G., Kerr, D. C. R., & Grandin, T. (1999). Behavioral and physiological effects of deep pressure on individuals with autism: A pilot study investigating the efficacy of Grandin's "Hug Machine." *American Journal of Occupational Therapy, 53,* 145–152.

Eisenmajer, R., Prior, M., Leekam, S., Wing, L., Gould, J., Welham, M., et al. (1996). Comparison of clinical symptoms in autism and Asperger's disorder. *Journal of the American Academy of Child and Adolescent Psychiatry, 35,* 1523–1531.

Eledevik, S., Eikeseth, S., Jahr, E., & Smith, T. (2006). Effects of low-intensity behavioral treatment for children with autism and mental retardation. *Journal of Autism and Developmental Disorders, 36,* 211–224.

Ermer, J., & Dunn, W. (1998). The Sensory Profile: A discriminant analysis of children with and without disabilities. *American Journal of Occupational Therapy, 52,* 283–290.

Escalona, A., Field, T., Singer-Strunck, R., Cullen C., & Hartshorn, K. (2001). Brief Report: Improvements in the behavior of children with autism following massage therapy. *Journal of Autism and Developmental Disorders, 31,* 513–516.

Fein, D., Humes, M., Kaplan, E., Lucci, D., & Waterhouse, L. (1984). The question of left-hemisphere dysfunction in infantile autism. *Psychological Bulletin, 95,* 258–281.

Field, T., Field, T., Sanders, C., & Nadel. J. (2001). Children with autism display more social behaviors after repeated imitation sessions. *Autism, 5,* 317–323.

Field, T., Lasko, D., Mundy, P., Henteleff, T., Kabat, S., Talpins, S., et al. (1997). Brief Report: Autistic children's attentiveness and responsivity improve after touch therapy. *Journal of Autism and Developmental Disorders, 27,* 333–338.

Filipek, P. A., Accardo, P. J., Ashwal, S., Baranek, G. T., Cook, Jr., E. H., Dawson, G., et al. (2000). Practice Parameter: Screening and diagnosis of autism (Report of the Quality Standards Subcommittee of the American Academy of Neurology and the Child Neurology Society). *Neurology, 55,* 468–479.

Filipek, P. A., Accardo, P. J., Baranek, G. T., Cook Jr., E. H., Dawson, G., & Gordon, B. (1999). The screening and diagnosis of autism spectrum disorders. *Journal of Autism and Developmental Disorders, 29,* 439–484.

Fisher, A. G., Bryze, K., Hume, V., & Griswold, L. A. (2005). *School AMPS: School Version of the Assessment of Motor and Process Skills* (2nd ed.). Fort Collins, CO: Three Star Press.

Fisman, S., Wolf, L., Ellison, D., Gillis, B., & Freeman, T. (2000). A longitudinal study of siblings of children with chronic disabilities. *Canadian Journal of Psychiatry, 45,* 369–375.

Fisman, S., Wolf, L., Ellison, D., Gillis, B., Freeman, T., & Szatmari, P. (1996). Risk and protective factors affecting the adjustment of siblings of children with chronic disabilities. *Journal of the American Academy of Child and Adolescent Psychiatry, 35,* 1532–1541.

Folio, R., & Fewell, R. (2000). *Peabody Developmental Motor Scales* (2nd ed.). Austin, TX: Pro-Ed.

Fombonne, E. (2003a). Epidemiological surveys of autism and other pervasive developmental disorders: An update. *Journal of Autism and Developmental Disorders, 33,* 365–382.

Fombonne, E. (2003b). The prevalence of autism. *JAMA, 289,* 87–89.

Frick, S. M., & Hacker, C. (2001). *Listening with the whole body.* Madison, WI: Vital Links.

Gardner, M. F. (1995). *Test of Visual–Motor Skills–Revised (TVMS–R).* Los Angeles: Western Psychological Services.

Gardner, M. F. (1997). *Test of Visual Perceptual Skills–Upper Limits (TVPS–UL).* Los Angeles: Western Psychological Services.

Gardner, M. F. (1998). *Test of Handwriting Skills.* Los Angeles: Western Psychological Services.

Gepner, B., & Mestre, D. R. (2002). Brief Report: Postural reactivity to fast visual motion differentiates autistic children from children with Asperger syndrome. *Journal of Autism and Developmental Disorders, 32,* 231–238.

Gepner, B., Mestre, D. R., Masson, G., & de Schonen, S. (1995). Postural effects of motion vision in young autistic children. *Neuro-Report, 6,* 1211–1214.

Gevers, C., Clifford, P., Mager, M., & Boer, F. (2006). Brief Report: A theory-of-mind–based social–cognition training program for school-aged children with pervasive developmental disorders: An open study of its effectiveness. *Journal of Autism and Developmental Disorders, 36,* 567–571.

Ghaziuddin, M., Ghaziuddin, N., & Greden, J. (2002). Depression in persons with autism: Implications for research and clinical care. *Journal of Autism and Developmental Disorders, 32*(4), 299–306.

Ghaziuddin, M., Tsai, L. Y., & Ghaziuddin, N. (1992). Brief Report: A reappraisal of clumsiness as a diagnostic feature of Asperger syndrome. *Journal of Autism and Developmental Disorders, 22,* 651–656.

Gillberg, C., & Coleman, M. (1996). Autism and medical disorders: A review of literature. *Developmental Medicine and Child Neurology, 38,* 191–202.

Gillberg, C., & Coleman, M. (2000). *The biology of the autistic syndromes.* London: Cambridge Press.

Gillberg, C., Ehlers, S., Schaumann, H., Jakobsson, G., Dahlgren, S. O., Lindblom, R., et al. (1990). Autism under age 3 years: A clinical study of 28 cases referred for autistic symptoms in infancy. *Journal of Child Psychology and Psychiatry, 31,* 921–934.

Gioia, G. A., Inquish, P. K., Guy, S. C., & Kenworthy, L. (2000). *The Behavior Rating Inventory of Executive Function.* Lutz, FL: Psychological Assessment Resources.

Glover, E. M., Preminger, J. L., & Sanford, A. R. (1998). *Early Learning Accomplishment Profile, Revised Edition (E–LAP).* Lewisville, NC: Kaplan Press.

Gold, N. (1993). Depression and social adjustment in siblings of boys with autism. *Journal of Autism and Developmental Disorders, 23,* 147–163.

Graetz, J. E., & Spampinato, K. (2008, Winter). Asperger's syndrome and the voyage through high school: Not the final frontier. *Journal of College Admission, 1,* 19–24.

Grandin, T. (1992). An inside view of autism. In E. Schopler & G. B. Mesibov (Eds.), *High functioning individuals with autism* (pp. 105–126). New York: Plenum.

Grandin, T. (1995). *Thinking in pictures*. New York: Doubleday.

Grandin, T., & Scariano, N. M. (1986). *Emergence: Labeled autistic*. Novato, CA: Arena Press.

Gray, C. (2000). *The new social story book*. Arlington, TX: Future Horizons.

Greene, S. (2004). Social skills intervention for children with an autism spectrum disorder. In H. Miller Kuhaneck (Ed.), *Autism: A comprehensive occupational therapy approach* (2nd ed., pp. 171–192). Bethesda, MD: AOTA Press.

Greenspan, S. I., & Wieder, S. (1997). Developmental patterns and outcomes in infants and children with disorders in relating and communicating: A chart review of 200 cases of children with autistic spectrum diagnoses. *Journal of Developmental and Learning Disorders, 1,* 87–142.

Greenspan, S. I., & Wieder, S. (2006). *Engaging autism: Using the floortime approach to help children relate, communicate, and think.* New York: Da Capo Press.

Gudmundson, E. (1993). Lateral preference of preschool and primary school children. *Perceptual and Motor Skills, 77,* 819–828.

Haas, R. H., Townsend, J., Courchesne, E., Lincoln, A. J., Schriebman, L., & Yeung-Courchesne, R. (1996). Neurological abnormalities in infantile autism. *Journal of Child Neurology, 11,* 84–92.

Haley, S. M., Coster, W. J., Ludlow, L. H., Haltiwanger, J. T., & Andrellos, P. J. (1992). *Pediatric Evaluation of Disability Inventory: Development, standardization, and administration manual, version 1.0.* Boston: Trustees of Boston University, Health and Disability Research Institute.

Hall, L., & Case-Smith, J. (2007). The effect of sound-based intervention on children with sensory processing disorders and visual–motor delays. *American Journal of Occupational Therapy, 61,* 209–215.

Hallett, M., Lebiedowska, M. K., Thomas, S. L., Stanhope, S. J., Denckla, M. B., & Rumsey, J. (1993).

Locomotion of autistic adults. *Archives of Neurology, 50,* 1304–1308.

Hammill, D. D., Pearson, N. A., & Voress, J. K. (1993). *Developmental Test of Visual Perception* (2nd ed.). Austin, TX: Pro-Ed.

Hanft, B. E., Rush, D. D., & Sheldon, M. L. (2003). *Coaching families and colleagues in early childhood.* Baltimore: Paul H. Brookes.

Harrison, P., & Oakland, T. (2003). *Adaptive Behavior Assessment System* (2nd ed.). San Antonio, TX: Harcourt.

Hartishorn, K., Olds, L., Field, T., Delage, J., Cullen, C., & Escalona, A. (2001). Creative movement therapy benefits children with autism. *Early Child Development and Care, 186,* 1–8.

Hassall, R., Rose, J., & McDonald, J. (2005). Parenting stress in mothers of children with an intellectual disability: The effects of parental cognitions in relation to child characteristics and family support. *Journal of Intellectual Disability Research, 49,* 405–418.

Hauck, J. A., & Dewey, D. (2001). Hand preference and motor functioning in children with autism. *Journal of Autism and Developmental Disorders, 31,* 265–277.

Horner, R., Carr, E., Strain, P., Todd, A., & Reed, H. (2002). Problem behavior interventions for young children. *Journal of Autism and Developmental Disorders, 32,* 423–446.

Hoshino, Y., Kumashiro, H., Yashima, Y., Tachibana, R., Watanabe, M., & Furukawa, H. (1982). Early symptoms of autistic children and its diagnostic significance. *Folia Psychiatrica et Neurologica Japonica, 36,* 367–374.

Howlin, P., & Yates. P. (1999). The potential effectiveness of social skills group for adults with autism. *Autism, 3,* 299–307.

Hughes, C. (1996). Brief Report: Planning problems in autism at the level of motor control. *Journal of Autism and Developmental Disorders, 26,* 99–107.

Hughes, C., & Russell, J. (1993). Autistic children's difficulty with mental disengagement from an object: Its implications for theories in autism. *Developmental Psychology, 29,* 498–510.

Hurth, J., Shaw, E., Izeman, S., Whaley, K., & Rogers, S. (1999). Areas of agreement about effective practices among programs serving young children with ASDs. *Infants and Young Children, 12,* 17–26.

Hwang, B., & Hughes, C. (2000). The effects of social interactive training on early social communicative skills of children with autism. *Journal of Autism and Developmental Disorders, 30,* 331–343.

Individuals With Disabilities Education Act of 1990. Pub. L. No. 101–476, 20 U.S.C., Ch. 33.

Individuals With Disabilities Education Improvement Act. (2004). Pub. L No. 108-448.

Jocelyn, L. J., Casiro, O. G., Beattie, D., Bow, J., & Kneisz, J. (1998). Treatment of children with autism: A randomized controlled trial to evaluate a caregiver-based intervention program in community day-care centers. *Developmental and Behavioral Pediatrics, 19,* 326–334.

Johnson, C. P., Myers, S. M., & Council on Children With Disabilities. (2007). Identification and evaluation of children with autism spectrum disorders. *Pediatrics, 5,* 1183–1215.

Jones, V., & Prior, M. (1985). Motor imitation abilities and neurological signs in autistic children. *Journal of Autism and Developmental Disorders, 15,* 37–46.

Kabot, S., Masi, W., & Segal, M. (2003). Advances in the diagnosis and treatment of autism spectrum disorders. *Professional Psychology: Research and Practice, 34,* 26–33.

Kanner, L. (1943). Autistic disturbances of affective contact. *Nervous Child, 2,* 217–250.

Kasari, C., Freeman, S., & Paparella, T. (2006). Joint attention and symbolic play in young children with autism: A randomized controlled intervention study. *Journal of Child Psychology and Psychiatry and Allied Disciplines, 4,* 611–620.

Kielinen, M., Rantala, H., Timonen, E., Linna, S. L., & Moilanen, I. (2004). Associated medical disorders and disabilities in children with autistic disorder: A population-based study. *Autism, 8,* 49–60.

Kientz, M. A., & Dunn, W. (1997). A comparison of the performance of children with and without autism on the Sensory Profile. *American Journal of Occupational Therapy, 51,* 530–537.

Kientz, M. A., & Miller, H. (1999, March). Classroom evaluation of the child with autism. *School System Special Interest Section Quarterly, 6,* 1–4.

Kientz, M., & Miller-Kuhaneck, H. (2001). Occupational therapy evaluation of the child with autism. In H. Miller-Kuhaneck (Ed.), *Autism: A comprehensive occupational therapy approach* (pp 55–84). Bethesda, MD: American Occupational Therapy Association.

King, G., Law, M., King, S., Hurley, P., Rosenbaum, P., Hanna, S., et al. (2005). *Children's Assessment of Participation and Enjoyment (CAPE) and Preferences for Activities of Children (PAC).* San Antonio, TX: Harcourt.

Klin, A., Volkmar, F. R., & Sparrow, S. S. (1992). Autistic social dysfunction: Some limitations of the theory of mind hypothesis. *Journal of Child Psychology and Psychiatry, 33,* 861–876.

Klin, A., Volkmar, R. R., Sparrow, S. S., Cicchetti, D. V., & Rourke, B. P. (1995). Validity and neuropsychological characterization of Asperger syndrome: Convergence with nonverbal learning disabilities syndrome. *Journal of Child Psychology and Psychiatry, 36,* 1127–1140.

Knox, S. (2008). Development and current use of the Knox Preschool Play Scale. In L. Parham & L. Fazio (Eds.), *Play in occupational therapy for children* (pp. 55–70). St. Louis, MO: Mosby/Year Book.

Koegel, R. L., Bimbela, A., & Schreibman, L. (1996). Collateral effects of parent training on family interactions. *Journal of Autism and Developmental Disorders, 26,* 347–359.

Koegel, R. L., Koegel, L. K., & Carter, C. M. (1999). Pivotal teaching interactions for children with autism. *School Psychology Review, 28,* 576–594.

Koegel, L. K., Koegel, R. L., & Smith, A. (1997). Variables related to differences in standardized test scores. *Journal of Autism and Developmental Disorders, 27,* 233–243.

Kohen-Raz, R., Volkmar, F. R., & Cohen, D. J. (1992). Postural control in children with autism. *Journal of Autism and Developmental Disorders, 22,* 419–432.

Law, M., Baptiste, S., Carswell, A., McColl, M. A., Polatajko, H., & Pollock, N. (2005). *Canadian Occupational Performance Measure* (4th ed.). Ottawa: CAOT Publications.

Law, M., Baptiste, S., Carswell-Opzoomer, A., McColl, M. A., Polatajko, H., & Pollock, N. (1994). *Canadian Occupational Performance Measure* (2nd ed.). Ottawa: CAOT Publications.

Law, M., & Baum, C. (1998). Evidence-based occupational therapy. *Canadian Journal of Occupational Therapy, 65,* 131–135.

Leary, M., & Hill, D. (1996). Moving on: Autism and movement disturbance. *Mental Retardation, 34,* 39–53.

LeCouteur, A., Rutter, M., Lord, C., Rios, P., Robertson, S., Holdgrafer, M., et al. (1989). Autism Diagnostic Interview: A standardized investigator-based instrument. *Journal of Autism and Developmental Disorders, 19,* 363–387.

LeGoff, D. B. (2004). Use of LEGO as a therapeutic medium for improving social competence. *Journal of Autism and Developmental Disorders, 34,* 557–571.

LeGoff, D. B., & Sherman, M. (2006). Long-term outcome of social skills intervention based on interactive LEGO play. *Autism, 1,* 317–329.

Levy, S. E., & Hyman, S. L. (2003). Use of complementary and alternative treatments for children with autistic spectrum disorders is increasing. *Pediatric Annals, 32,* 685–691.

Lincoln, A. J., Courchesne, E., Harms, L., & Allen, M. (1995). Contextual probability evaluation in autistic, receptive developmental language disorder, and control children: Event-related brain potential evidence. *Journal of Autism and Developmental Disorders, 23,* 37–58.

Linder, T. W. (2008). *Transdisciplinary Play-Based Assessment: A functional approach to working with young children* (2nd ed.). Baltimore: Paul H. Brookes.

Linderman, T. M., & Stewart, K. B. (1999). Sensory integrative-based occupational therapy and functional outcomes in young children with pervasive developmental disorders: A single-subject study. *American Journal of Occupational Therapy, 53,* 207–213.

Lord, C. (1995). Follow-up of two-year-olds referred for possible autism. *Journal of Child Psychology and Psychiatry, 36,* 1365–1382.

Lord, C., & Risi, S. (2000). Diagnosis of autism spectrum disorders in young children. In A. M. Wetherby & B. M. Prizant (Eds.), *Autism spectrum disorders: A transactional developmental perspective* (pp. 167–190). Baltimore: Paul H. Brookes.

Lord, C., Rutter, M., DiLavore, P. C., & Risi, S. (2002). *Autism Diagnostic Observation Schedule.* Los Angeles: Western Psychological Services.

Lord, C., Rutter, M., & LeCouteur, A. (1994). Autism Diagnostic Interview–Revised: A revised version of the diagnostic interview for caregivers of individuals with possible pervasive developmental disorder. *Journal of Autism and Developmental Disorders, 24,* 659–685.

Lord, C., Schopler, E., & Revicki, D. (1982). Sex differences in autism. *Journal of Autism and Developmental Disorders, 12,* 317–330.

Losche, G. (1990). Sensorimotor and action development in autistic children from infancy to early childhood. *Journal of Child Psychology and Psychiatry, 31,* 749–761.

Lovaas, O. (1987). Behavioral treatment and normal educational and intellectual functioning in young autistic children. *Journal of Consultation and Clinical Psychology, 55,* 359–372.

Luiselli, J. K., Cannon, B. O., Ellis, J. T., & Sisson, R. W. (2000). Home-based behavioral intervention for young children with autism/pervasive developmental disorder. *Autism, 4,* 426–438.

MacDonald, J. (1989). *Becoming partners with children: From play to conversation.* San Antonio, TX: Special Press.

Mahoney, G., & Perales, F. (2005). Relationship-focused early intervention with children with pervasive developmental disorders and other disabilities: A comparative study. *Developmental and Behavioral Pediatrics, 26,* 77–85.

Mailloux, Z. (2001). Sensory integrative principles in intervention with children with autistic disorder. In S. Roley, E. Blanche, & R. Schaaf (Eds.), *Understanding the nature of sensory integration with diverse populations* (pp. 365–384). San Antonio, TX: Psychological Corporation.

Mailloux, Z., & Roley, S. S. (2004). Sensory integration. In H. Miller-Kuhaneck (Ed.), *Autism: A comprehensive occupational therapy approach* (2nd ed., pp. 215–244). Bethesda, MD: AOTA Press.

Manjiviona, J., & Prior, M. (1995). Comparison of Asperger syndrome and high-functioning autistic children on a test of motor impairment. *Journal of Autism and Developmental Disorders, 25,* 23–39.

Mari, M., Castiello, U., Marks, D., Marraffa, C., & Prior, M. (2003). The reach-to-grasp movement in children with autism spectrum disorder. *Philosophical Transactions of the Royal Society of London, Series B, Biological Sciences, 358,* 393–403.

Martin, N. A. (2006). *Test of Visual Perceptual Skills* (3rd ed.). Los Angeles: Western Psychological Services.

Matson, J. L., & Nebel-Schwalm, M. S. (2007). Comorbid psychopathology with autism spectrum disorder in children: An overview. *Research in Developmental Disabilities, 28,* 341–352.

Maurer, R. G., & Damasio, A. G. (1982). Childhood autism from the point of view of behavioral neurology. *Journal of Autism and Developmental Disorders, 12,* 195–205.

Mayes, S. D., & Calhoun, S. L. (1999). Symptoms of autism in young children and correspondence with the *DSM. Infants and Young Children, 12,* 90–97.

McEachie, J. J., Smith, T., & Lovaas, O. (1993). Long-term outcome for children with autism who received early intensive behavioral treatment. *American Journal of Mental Retardation, 97,* 350–372.

McEvoy, R. E., Rogers, S. J., & Pennington, B. F. (1993). Executive function and social communication deficits in young autistic children. *Journal of Child Psychology and Psychiatry, 34,* 563–578.

McGee, G. G., Morrier, M. J., & Daly, T. (1999). An incidental teaching approach to early intervention for toddlers with autism. *Journal of the Association for Persons With Severe Handicaps, 24,* 133–146.

McIntosh, D. N., Miller, L. J., & Shyu, V. (1999). Development and validation of the Short Sensory Profile. In W. Dunn (Ed.), *The Sensory Profile examiner's manual* (pp. 59–73). San Antonio, TX: Psychological Corporation.

McLennan, J. D., Lord, C., & Schopler, E. (1993). Sex differences in higher functioning people with autism. *Journal of Autism and Developmental Disorders, 23,* 217–227.

McManus, I. C., Murray, B., Doyle, K., & Baron-Cohen, S. (1982). Handedness in childhood autism shows a dissociation of skill and preference. *Cortex, 28,* 373–381.

McWilliam, R. A. (1991). *Children's Engagement Questionnaire.* Nashville, TN: Author, Vanderbilt Center of Child Development.

McWilliam, R. A., & Bailey, D. B. (1992). Promoting engagement and mastery. In M. Wolery (Ed.), *Teaching infants and preschoolers with disabilities* (pp. 230–255). New York: MacMillan.

McWilliam, R. A., Trivette, C. M., & Dunst, C. J. (1985). Behavior engagement as a measure of the efficacy of early intervention. *Analysis and Intervention in Developmental Disabilities, 5,* 59–71.

Miller, H. (1996, June). Eye contact and gaze aversion: Implications for persons with autism. *Sensory Integration Special Interest Section Quarterly, 19*(2), 1–3.

Miller, L. J. (2006). *Miller Function and Participation Scales manual.* San Antonio, TX: Pearson.

Miller, L. J., Anzalone, X., Lane, S. J., Cermak, S. A., & Osten, E. T. (2007). Concept evolution in sensory integration: A proposed nosology for diagnosis. *American Journal of Occupational Therapy, 61,* 135–140.

Miller, L. J., & Lane, S. J. (2000, March). Towards a consensus in terminology in sensory integration theory and practice: Part one: Taxonomy of neuropsychological processes. *Sensory Integration Special Interest Section Quarterly, 23*(1), 1–4.

Miller, L. J., Reisman, J., McIntosh, D., & Simon, J. (2001). An ecological model of sensory modulation. In S. Smith Roley, E. Blanche, & R. C. Schaaf (Eds.), *Understanding the nature of sensory integration with diverse populations* (pp. 57–85). Los Angeles: Harcourt.

Miller, L. J., & Summers, C. (2001). Clinical applications in sensory modulation dysfunction: Assessment and intervention considerations. In S. Smith Roley, E. Blanche, & R. C. Schaaf (Eds.), *Understanding the nature of sensory integration with diverse populations* (pp. 247–273). Los Angeles: Harcourt.

Miller-Kuhaneck, H., Henry, D., & Glennon, T. (2007). *Sensory Processing Measure, Main Classroom and School Environment Forms.* Los Angeles: Western Psychological Services.

Minshew, N. J., Goldstein, G., & Siegel, D. J. (1997). Neuropsychologic functioning in autism: Profile of a complex information processing disorder. *Journal of the International Neurophysiological Society, 3,* 303–316.

Missiuna, C., Pollock, N., & Law, M. (2004). *Perceived Efficacy and Goal Setting System (PEGS).* Oxford, UK: Harcourt Assessment.

Miyahara, M., Tsujii, M., Hori, M., Nakanishi, K., Kageyama, H., & Sugiyama, T. (1997). Brief Report: Motor incoordination in children with Asperger syndrome and learning disabilities. *Journal of Autism and Developmental Disorders, 27,* 595–603.

Moyers, P., & Dale, L. (2007). *The guide to occupational therapy practice* (2nd ed.). Bethesda, MD: AOTA Press.

Mudford, O. C., Cross, B. A., Breen, S., Cullen, C., Reeves, D., Gould, J., et al. (2000). Auditory integration training for children with autism: No behavioral benefits detected. *American Journal on Mental Retardation, 105,* 118–129.

Myers, S. M., Johnson, C. P., & Council on Children With Disabilities. (2007). Management of children with autism spectrum disorders. *Pediatrics, 5,* 1162–1182.

Nass, R., & Gutman, R. (1997). Boys with Asperger's disorder, exceptional verbal intelligence, and clumsiness. *Developmental Medicine and Child Neurology, 39,* 691–695.

National Research Council. (2001). *Educating children with autism.* Washington, DC: National Academy Press.

Nelson, D. L. (1982). Evaluating autistic clients. *Occupational Therapy in Mental Health, 1,* 1–22.

Newborg, J. (2004). *Battelle Developmental Inventory– Second Edition manual.* Rolling Meadows, IL: Riverside.

Ohta, M. (1987). Cognitive disorders of infantile autism: A study employing the WISC, spatial relationship conceptualization, and gesture imitations. *Journal of Autism and Developmental Disorders, 17,* 45–62.

Olsson, M. B., & Hwang, C. P. (2001). Depression in mothers and fathers of children with intellectual disability. *Journal of Intellectual Disability Research, 45,* 535–543.

Ornitz, E. M. (1989). Autism at the interface between sensory and information processing. In G. Dawson (Ed.), *Autism: Nature, diagnosis, and treatment* (pp. 174–207). New York: Guilford Press.

Ornitz, E. M., Guthrie, D., & Farley, A. H. (1977). The early development of autistic children. *Journal of Autism and Developmental Disorders, 7,* 207–229.

Ornitz, E. M., Guthrie, D., & Farley, A. H. (1978). The early symptoms of childhood autism. In G. Sherban (Ed.), *Cognitive defects in the development of mental illness* (pp. 207–299). New York: Brunner/Mazel.

Ornitz, E. M., Lane, S. J., Sugiyama, T., & de Traversay, J. (1993). Startle modulation studies in autism. *Journal of Autism and Developmental Disorders, 23,* 619–637.

Osterling, J., & Dawson, G. (1994). Early recognition of children with autism: A study of first birthday home videotapes. *Journal of Autism and Developmental Disorders, 24,* 247–257.

Ozonoff, S., & Cathcart, K. (1998). Effectiveness of a home program intervention for young children with autism. *Journal of Autism and Developmental Disorders, 28,* 25–32.

Ozonoff, S., Goodlin-Jones, B. L., & Solomon, M. (2005). Evidenced-based assessment of autism spectrum disorders in children and adolescents. *Journal of Clinical Child and Adolescent Psychology, 34,* 523–540.

Ozonoff, S., & Miller, J. (1995). Teaching theory of mind: A new approach to social skills training for individuals with autism. *Journal of Autism and Developmental Disorders, 25,* 415–433.

Panerai, S., Ferrante, L., & Zingale, M. (2002). Benefits of the Treatment and Education of Autistic and Communication Handicapped Children (TEACCH) programme as compared with a non-specific approach. *Journal of Intellectual Disability Research, 46,* 318–327.

Parham, D., Cohn, E. S., Spitzer, S., Koomar, J. A., Miller, L. J., Burke, J. P., et al. (2007). Fidelity in sensory integration intervention research. *American Journal of Occupational Therapy, 61,* 216–227.

Parham, D., & Ecker, C. (2007). *Sensory Processing Measure, Home Form.* Los Angeles: Western Psychological Services.

Parham, D., & Mailloux, Z. (2005). Sensory integration. In J. Case-Smith (Ed.), *Occupational therapy with children* (pp. 356–411). St. Louis, MO: Mosby/Elsevier.

Prior, M. (2003). Is there an increase in the prevalence of ASDs? *Journal of Paediatric Child Health, 39,* 81–82.

Prizant, B. M., & Wetherby, A. M. (1993). Communication in preschool autistic children. In E. Schopler, M. E. Van Bourgondien, & M. M. Bristol (Eds.), *Preschool issues in autism* (pp. 95–128). New York: Plenum Press.

Provost, B., Heimerl, S., & Lopez, B. R. (2007). Levels of gross and fine motor development in young children with autism spectrum disorder. *Physical and Occupational Therapy in Pediatrics, 27*(3), 21–36.

Provost, B., Lopez, B. R., & Heimerl, S. (2006). A comparison of motor delays in young children: Autism spectrum disorder, developmental delay, and developmental concerns. *Journal of Autism and Developmental Disorders, 37,* 321–328.

Rapin, I. (1991). Autistic children: Diagnosis and clinical features. *Pediatrics, 87,* 751–760.

Rapin, I. (1996). Neurologic examination. In I. Rapin (Ed.), *Preschool children with inadequate communication: Developmental language disorder, autism, low IQ.* London: MacKeith Press.

Redefer, L. A., & Goodman, J. F. (1989). Brief Report: Pet-facilitated therapy with autistic children. *Journal of Autism and Developmental Disorders, 19,* 461–467.

Reiersen, A. M., & Todd, R. D. (2008). Co-occurrence of ADHD and autism spectrum disorders: Phenomenology and treatment. *Expert Review of Neurotherapeutics, 8,* 657–669.

Reinhartsen, D. B., Garfinkle, A. N., & Wolery, M. (2002). Engagement with toys in two-year-old children with autism: Teacher selection versus child choice. *Research and Practice for Persons With Severe Disabilities, 27,* 175–187.

Reisman, J. E. (1999). *Minnesota Handwriting Assessment user's manual.* San Antonio, TX: Psychological Corporation.

Reisman, J. E., & Hanschu, B. (1992). *Sensory Integration Inventory–Revised for individuals with developmental disabilities: User's guide.* Hugo, MN: PDP Press.

Reynhout, G., & Carter, M. (2006). Social Stories for children with disabilities. *Journal of Autism and Developmental Disorders, 36,* 445–469.

Reynolds, C. R., Pearson, N. A., & Voress, J. K. (2002). *Developmental Test of Visual Perception–Adolescent and Adult (DTVP–A).* Lutz, FL: Psychological Assessment Resources.

Rimland, B., & Edelson, S. M. (1995). Brief Report: A pilot study of auditory integration training in autism. *Journal of Autism and Developmental Disorders, 25,* 61–70.

Rinehart, N. J., Bradshaw, J. L., Brereton, A. V., & Tonge, B. J. (2001). Movement preparation in high-functioning autism and Asperger disorder: A serial choice reaction time task involving motor reprogramming. *Journal of Autism and Developmental Disorders, 31,* 79–88.

Rogers, S. J., Bennetto, L., McEvoy, R., & Pennington, B. F. (1996). Imitation and pantomime in high-functioning adolescents with ASDs. *Child Development, 67,* 2060–2073.

Rogers, S. J., & DiLalla, D. L. (1991). A comparative study of the effects of a developmentally based instructional model on young children with autism and young children with other disorders of behavior and development. *Topics in Early Childhood Special Education, 11*(2), 29–47.

Rogers, S. J., Hepburn, S., & Wehner, E. (2003). Parent reports of sensory symptoms in toddlers with autism and those with other developmental disorders. *Journal of Autism and Developmental Disorders, 33,* 631–642.

Rogers, S. J., Herbison, J. M., Lewis, H. C., Pantone, J., & Rels, K. (1986). An approach for enhancing the symbolic communicative and interpersonal functioning of young children with autism or severe emotional handicaps. *Journal of the Division for Early Childhood, 10*(2), 135–148.

Rogers, S. J., Wehner, D. E., & Hagerman, R. (2001). The behavioral phenotype in Fragile X: Symptoms of autism in very young children with Fragile X syndrome, idiopathic autism, and other developmental disorders. *Journal of Developmental and Behavioral Pediatrics, 22,* 409–417.

Ross, P., & Cuskelly, M. (2006). Adjustment, sibling problems, and coping strategies of brothers and sisters of children with autistic spectrum disorder. *Journal of Intellectual and Developmental Disability, 31*(2), 77–86.

Ruble, L. A., & Dalrymple, N. J. (1996). An alternative view of outcome in autism. *Focus on Autism and Other Developmental Disabilities, 11,* 3–14.

Ruble, L. A., & Dalrymple, N. J. (2002). COMPASS: A parent–teacher collaborative model for students with autism. *Focus on Autism and Other Developmental Disabilities, 17,* 76–83.

Ruble, L. A., & Robson, D. (2007). Individual and environmental determinants of engagement in autism. *Journal of Autism and Developmental Disorders, 37,* 1457–1468.

Rumsey, J. M., & Hamburger, S. D. (1990). Neuropsychological divergence of high-level autism and severe dyslexia. *Journal of Autism and Developmental Disorders, 20,* 155–168.

Rutter, M. (2005). Incidence of autism spectrum disorders: Changes over time and their meaning. *Acta Paediatrica, 94,* 2–15.

Rutter, M., & Schopler, E. (1988). Autism and pervasive developmental disorders: Concepts and diagnostic issues. In E. Schopler & G. Mesibov (Eds.), *Diagnosis and assessment in autism* (pp. 15–35). New York: Plenum Press.

Sackett, D. L., Rosenberg, W. M., Muir Gray, J. A., Haynes, R. B., & Richardson, W. S. (1996). Evidence-based medicine: What it is and what it isn't. *British Medical Journal, 312,* 71–72.

Sallows, G. O., & Graupner, T. D. (2005). Intensive behavioral treatment for children with autism: Four-year outcome and predictors. *American Journal on Mental Retardation, 110,* 417–438.

Salt, J., Shemilt, J., Sellars, V., Boyd, S., Coulson, T., & McCool, S. (2001). The Scottish Centre for autism preschool treatment programme I: A developmental approach to early intervention. *Autism, 5,* 362–373.

Salt, J., Shemilt, J., Sellars, V., Boyd, S., Coulson, T., & McCool, S. (2002). The Scottish Centre for autism preschool treatment programme II: The results of a controlled treatment outcome study. *Autism, 6,* 34–46.

Sanders, J. L., & Morgan, S. B. (1997). Family stress and adjustment as perceived by parents of children with autism or Down syndrome: Implications for intervention. *Child and Family Behavior Therapy, 19*(4), 15–32.

Sanford, A. R., & Zelman, J. G. (1981). *The Learning Accomplishment Profile (LAP).* Winston-Salem, NC: Kaplan Press.

Satz, P., Green, M. F., & Lyon, N. (1989). Some pathological substrates in manual laterality. *Brain Dysfunction, 2,* 25–33.

Satz, P., Soper, H. V., Orsini, D. L., Henry, R. R., & Zvi, J. C. (1985). Human hand preference: Three nondextral subtypes. In D. C. Molfese & S. J. Segalowitz (Eds.), *Brain lateralization in children: Developmental implications* (pp. 281–287). New York: Guilford.

Schleien, S. J., Mustonen, T., & Rynders, J. E. (1995). Participation of children with autism and nondisabled peers in a cooperatively structured community art program. *Journal of Autism and Developmental Disorders, 25,* 397–413.

Schleien, S. J., Mustonen, T., Rynders, J. E., & Fox, A. (1990). Effects of social play activities on the play behavior of children with autism. *Journal of Leisure Research, 22,* 317–328.

Schopler, E., Mesibov, G. B., & Hearsey, K. (1995). Structured teaching in the TEACCH system. In G. B. Mesibov (Ed.), *Learning and cognition in autism: Current issues in autism* (pp. 243–268). New York: Plenum Press.

Schopler, E., Mesibov, G. B., Shigley, R. H., & Bashford, A. (1984). Helping autistic children through their parents: The TEACCH model. In E. Schopler & G. B. Mesibov (Eds.), *The effects of autism on the family* (pp. 65–81). New York: Plenum Press.

Schopler, E., Reichler, R. J., Bashford, A., Lansing, M., & Marcus, L. (1990). *The Psychoeducational Profile Revised (PEP–R).* Austin: Pro-Ed.

Schopler, E., Reichler, R. J., & Lansing, M. (1980). Assessment and evaluation. In E. Schopler, R. J. Reichler, & M. Lansing (Eds.), *Individualized assessment and treatment for autistic and developmentally disabled children: Teaching strategies for parents and professionals* (Vol. 2, pp. 23–41). Austin, TX: Pro-Ed.

Shelton, T. L., & Stepanek, J. S. (1994). *Family-centered care for children needing specialized health and developmental services.* Bethesda, MD: Association for the Care of Children's Health.

Sinha, Y., Silove, N., Wheeler, D., & Williams, K. (2005). Auditory integration training and other sound therapies for autism spectrum disorders. *Cochrane Database of Systematic Reviews,* Issue 1. Art No.: CD003681. DOI: 10.1002/14651858. CD003681 pub2.

Skard, G., & Bundy, A. (2008). Test of Playfulness. In L. D. Parham & L. S. Fazio (Eds.), *Play in occupational therapy for children* (2nd ed., pp. 71–94). St Louis, MO: Elsevier/Mosby.

Smalley, S. L. (1998). Autism and tuberous sclerosis. *Journal of Autism and Developmental Disorders, 28,* 407–414.

Smith, C., Goddard, S., & Fluck, M. (2004). A scheme to promote social attention and functional language in young children with communication difficulties and autistic spectrum disorder. *Educational Psychology in Practice, 20,* 319–334.

Smith, S. E., & Bryson, I. M. (1998). Epidemiology of autism: Prevalence, associated characteristics, and implications for research and service delivery. *Mental Retardation and Developmental Disabilities Research Reviews, 4,* 97–103.

Smith, T., Groen, A. D., & Wynn, J. W. (2000). Randomized trial of intensive early intervention for children with pervasive developmental disorder. *American Journal on Mental Retardation, 105,* 269–285.

Smith, T., Lovaas, N. W., & Lovaas, O. I. (2002). Behaviors of children with high-functioning autism when paired with typically developing versus delayed peers: A preliminary study. *Behavioral Interventions, 17,* 129–143.

Sofronoff, K., & Farbotko, M. (2002). The effectiveness of parent management training to increase self-efficacy in parents of children with Asperger syndrome. *Autism, 6,* 271–286.

Sofronoff, K., Leslie, A., & Brown, W. (2004). Parent management training and Asperger syndrome. *Autism, 8,* 301–317.

Soper, H. V., Satz, P., Orsini, D. L., Henry, R. R., Zvi, J. C., & Schulman, M. (1986). Handedness patterns in autism suggest subtypes. *Journal of Autism and Developmental Disorders, 16,* 155–167.

Sparrow, S. S., Balla, D. A., & Cicchetti, D. V. (1984). *Vineland Adaptive Behavior Scales* (2nd ed.). Circle Pines, MN: American Guidance Service.

Sparrow, S. S., Cicchetti, D. V., & Balla, D. A. (2005). *Vineland Adaptive Behavior Scales* (2nd ed.). San Antonio, TX: Pearson.

Spitzer, S. L. (2003a). Using participant observation to study the occupations of young children with autism and other developmental disabilities. *American Journal of Occupational Therapy, 57*(1), 66–76.

Spitzer, S. L. (2003b). With and without words: Exploring occupation in relation to young children with autism. *Journal of Occupational Science, 10*(2), 67–79.

Spitzer, S. L. (2004). Common and uncommon daily activities in individuals with autism: Challenges and opportunities for supporting occupation. In H. Miller-Kuhaneck (Ed.), *Autism: A comprehensive occupational therapy approach* (2nd ed., pp. 83–106). Bethesda, MD: AOTA Press.

Spitzer, S. L. (2008). Play in children with autism: Structure and experience. In L. D. Parham & L. S. Fazio (Eds.), *Play in occupational therapy for children* (2nd ed., pp. 351–374). St. Louis, MO: Elsevier/Mosby.

Stone, W. L., Conrod, E. E., & Ousley, O. Y. (2000). Brief Report: Screening Tool for Autism in Two-Year-Olds (STAT): Development and preliminary data. *Journal of Autism and Developmental Disorders, 30,* 607–612.

Stone, W. L., & Lemanek, K. L. (1990). Parental report of social behaviors in autistic preschoolers. *Journal of Autism and Developmental Disorders, 20,* 513–522.

Stone, W. L., Lemanek, K. L., Fishel, P. T., Fernandez, M. C., & Altemeier, W. A. (1990). Play and imitation skills in the diagnosis of autism in young children. *Pediatrics, 86,* 267–272.

Stone, W. L., & Ousley, O. Y. (1996). Pervasive developmental disorders: Autism. In M. Wolraich (Ed.), *Disorders of development and learning: A practical guide to assessment and management* (2nd ed., pp. 379–405). Philadelphia: Mosby/YearBook.

Stone, W. L., Ousley, O. Y., Yoder, P. J., Hogan, K. L., & Hepburn, S. L. (1997). Non-verbal communication in two- and three-year-old children with autism. *Journal of Autism and Developmental Disorders, 27,* 677–696.

Strain, P., Wolery, M., & Izeman, S. (1998, Winter). Considerations for administrators in the design of service options for young children with autism and their families. *Young Exceptional Children,* pp. 8–16.

Sturm, H., Fernell, E., & Gilberg, C. (2004). Autism spectrum disorders in children with normal intellectual levels: Associated impairments and subgroups. *Developmental Medicine and Child Neurology, 46,* 444–447.

Szatmari, P., Bartolucci, G., & Bremner, R. (1989). Asperger's syndrome and autism: Comparison of early history and outcome. *Developmental Medicine and Child Neurology, 31,* 709–720.

Szatmari, P., Tuff, L., Finlayson, M. A., & Bartolucci, G. (1990). Asperger's syndrome and autism: Neurocognitive aspects. *Journal of the American Academy of Child and Adolescent Psychiatry, 29,* 130–136.

Tomchek, S. D., & Dunn, W. (2007). Sensory processing in children with and without autism: A comparative study using the Short Sensory Profile. *American Journal of Occupational Therapy, 61,* 190–200.

Trombly, C. (1995). Occupation: Purposefulness and meaningfulness as therapeutic mechanisms. *American Journal of Occupational Therapy, 49,* 960–972.

Turnbull, A. P., Turbiville, V., & Turnbull, H. R. (2000). Evolution of family–professional partnership models: Collective empowerment as the model for the early 21st century. In S. J. Meisels & J. P. Shonkoff (Eds.), *Handbook of early intervention* (pp. 640–650). New York: Cambridge University Press.

Uniform Data Systems. (2003). *The Wee Functional Independence Measure* (2nd ed.). Buffalo, NY: Author.

U.S. Department of Education. (1999). *Twenty-first annual report to Congress on the implementation of the Individuals with Disabilities Education Act.* Washington, DC: U.S. Government Printing Office.

U.S. Government Accountability Office. (2005). *Education of children with autism* (GOA-05-220 Special Education). Washington, DC: Author.

U.S. Office of Special Education Programs. (2006). *Monitoring, technical assistance, and enforcement.* 20 U.S.C. §§1416 and 1442.

U.S. Office of Special Education Programs. (n.d.). *National Technical Assistance Center on Positive Behavioral Interventions and Supports (PBIS).* Retrieved December 8, 2007, from http://www.pbis.org

Veenstra-Vanderweele, J., Christian, S. L., & Cook, E. H. Jr. (2004). Autism as a paradigmatic complex genetic disorder. *Annual Review of Genomics and Human Genetics, 5,* 379–405.

Vicker, B. A. (1993). Tracking facilitated communication and auditory integration training in Indiana: Hopes and outcomes. *In 1993 International Conference Proceedings: Autism: A world of options* (pp. 267–269). Bethesda, MD: Autism Society of America.

Vilensky, J. A., Damasio, A. R., & Maurer, R. G. (1981). Gait disturbances in patients with autistic behavior. *Archives of Neurology, 38,* 646–649.

Volkmar, F. R. (2000). Medical problems, treatments, and professionals. In M. D. Powers (Ed.), *Children with autism: A parent's guide* (2nd ed., pp. 73–74). Bethesda, MD: Woodbine House.

Volkmar, F. R., Cohen, D. J., & Paul, R. (1986). An evaluation of *DSM-III* criteria for infantile autism. *Journal of the American Academy of Child Psychiatry, 25,* 190–197.

Volkmar, F., Cook, E. H., Jr., Pomeroy, J., Realmuto, G., & Tanguay, P. (1999). American Academy of Child and Adolescent Psychiatry practice parameter for the assessment and treatment of children, adolescents, and adults with autism and other pervasive developmental disorders. *Journal of the American Academy of Child and Adolescent Psychiatry, 38*(Suppl.), 32S–54S.

Volkmar, F. R., Szatmari, P., & Sparrow, S. S. (1993). Sex differences in pervasive developmental disorders. *Journal of Autism and Developmental Disorders, 23,* 579–591.

Wainwright, L., & Fein, D. (1996). Play. In I. Rapin (Ed.), *Preschool children with inadequate communication* (pp. 173–189). Cambridge, UK: Cambridge University Press.

Watling, R. (2004). Behavioral and educational intervention approaches for the child with an autism spectrum disorder. In H. Miller Kuhaneck (Ed.), *Autism: A comprehensive occupational therapy approach* (2nd ed., pp. 245–274). Bethesda, MD: AOTA Press.

Watling, R. L., Deitz, J., & White, O. (2001). Comparison of Sensory Profile scores of young children with and without ASDs. *American Journal of Occupational Therapy, 55,* 416–423.

Watling, R., Tomchek, S., & LaVesser, P. (2005). The scope of occupational therapy services for individuals with autism spectrum disorders across the lifespan. *American Journal of Occupational Therapy, 59,* 680–683.

Watson, L. R., & Marcus, L. M. (1988). Diagnosis and assessment of preschool children. In E. Schopler & G. Mesibov (Eds.), *Diagnosis and assessment in autism* (pp. 271–301). New York: Plenum Press.

Werner, E., Dawson, G., Osterling, J., & Dinno, J. (2000). Recognition of ASDs before 1 year of age: A retrospective study based on home videotapes. *Journal of Autism and Developmental Disorders, 30,* 157–162.

Werner DeGrace, B. (2004). The everyday occupation of families with children with autism. *American Journal of Occupational Therapy, 58,* 543–550.

Wetherby, A. M., & Prizant, B. M. (2002). *Communication and Symbolic Behavior Scales–Developmental Profile.* Baltimore: Paul H. Brookes.

Wieder, S., & Greenspan, S. (2005). Can children with autism master the core deficits and become empathetic, creative, and reflective? *Journal of Developmental and Learning Disorders, 9,* 1–22.

Wilbarger, P., & Wilbarger, J. L. (1991). *Sensory defensiveness in children ages 2–12: An intervention guide for parents and other caretakers.* Santa Barbara, CA: Avanti Educational Programs.

Williams, D. (1995). *Somebody somewhere.* New York: Doubleday.

Wing, J. K. (1966). Diagnosis, epidemiology, aetilogy. In J. K. Wing (Ed.), *Early childhood autism: Clinical, educational, and social aspects* (pp. 3–50). London: Pergamon Press.

Wing, L. (1972). *Autistic children: A guide for parents and professionals.* Secaucus, NJ: Citadel Press.

Wing, L. (1980). *Early childhood autism.* London: Pergamon Press.

Wing, L. (1981). Asperger's syndrome: A clinical account. *Psychological Medicine, 11,* 115–129.

Wing, L., & Potter, D. (2002). The epidemiology of autistic spectrum disorders: Is the prevalence rising? *Mental Retardation and Developmental Disabilities Research Reviews, 8,* 151–161.

Wolery, M. (2000). Commentary: The environment as a source of variability: Implications for research with individuals who have autism. *Journal of Autism and Developmental Disorders, 30,* 379–381.

Wolery, M., & Garfinkle, A. N. (2002). Measures in intervention research with young children who have autism. *Journal of Autism and Developmental Disorders, 32,* 463–478.

Wolfberg, P. J. (1995). Enhancing children's play (Appendix: Play Preference Inventory). In K. A. Quill (Ed.), *Teaching children with autism: Strategies to enhance communication and socialization* (p. 217). Independence, KY: Thomson Delmar Learning.

Wong, V. (2006). Study of the relationship between tuberous sclerosis complex and autistic disorder. *Journal of Child Neurology, 21,* 199–204.

World Health Organization. (1980). *International statistical classification of diseases and related health problems.* Geneva: Author.

World Health Organization. (1994). *International classification of diseases: Diagnostic criteria for research* (10th ed.). Geneva: Author.

World Health Organization. (2001). *International classification of functioning, disability, and health.* Geneva: Author.

Yeung-Courchesne, R., & Courchesne, E. (1997). From impasse to insight in autism research: From behavioral symptoms to biological explanations. *Development and Psychopathology, 9,* 389–419.

Zollweg, W., Palm, D., & Vance, V. (1997). The efficacy of auditory integration training: A double blind study. *American Journal of Audiology, 6*(3), 39–47.